The Life Story
of an Otter

By the same author

JOHN PENROSE – A ROMANCE OF THE LAND'S END
(now republished in a new edition by CORNWALL EDITIONS)

THE LIFE STORY OF A BADGER
WILD LIFE AT THE LAND'S END
THE STORY OF A HARE
THE HISTORY OF A FOX
THE SMUGGLER'S DAUGHTER

J.C. TREGARTHEN

The Life Story of an Otter

CORNWALL EDITIONS LIMITED

FOWEY

CORNWALL EDITIONS LIMITED

8 Langurtho Road

Fowey Cornwall PL23 1EQ UK

01726 832483

www.cornwalleditions.co.uk

Publisher: Ian Grant

First published in London in 1909 by John Murray

This edition first published in the United Kingdom in 2005 by

Cornwall Editions Limited

ISBN 1-904-880-06-1

Front cover The Publishers wish to thank Martin Ridley for permission to reproduce his oil
painting, *Otter Youngster,* on the front cover of the book.

Typeset in Minion MM 367 Regular

Cover and text design by Asterisk Design and Editorial Solutions, Cornwall

Art Director: Roger Bristow

Editorial Director: Yvonne McFarlane

Editor: Luzette Strauss

Printed and bound in the United Kingdom by Short Run Press, Exeter

Papers used by Cornwall Editions are natural, recyclable products made from wood grown in
sustainable forests; the manufacturing processes conform to the environmental regulations
of the country of origin.

1 3 5 7 9 10 8 6 4

CONTENTS

❧

PREFACE TO THE ORIGINAL EDITION

ᴥᵹ

THE OTTER has long seemed to me worthy of serious attention, if only for the successful struggle it has waged against those exterminating agencies under which the badger, the wild-cat, the polecat and the marten have all but succumbed.

Its survival throughout Great Britain is due, partly to its endurance and resources when hunted and partly to qualities and habits which differentiate it from the other creatures of the wild. Its scent, for instance, unlike that of fox or badger, to which every tike and lurcher will stoop, is noticed by few dogs save hounds that have been trained to own it; and the outlawed beast thus gains a certain immunity from destruction.

Then the otter is a great wanderer, who not only traverses long stretches of coast and follows streams and rivers to their source, but crosses hills and even mountains to reach its fishing-grounds. It has been known to travel fifteen miles in a night, and not infrequently the holts where it lies up during the day are ten or twelve miles apart.

On the way to its quarters it will linger to fish or hunt, and the remains of eel, salmon, pike, rabbit, moorhen or wild-duck mark the scene of the midnight feast. But no matter how much it may leave uneaten the otter never returns to a kill, and so escapes the traps with which gamekeeper or water-bailiff is sure to ring the ground about it. Unlike its congener the polecat, the otter does not hoard food; unless the caches of frogs occasionally found in marshes are its work, and not that of the heron as is generally supposed.

However that may be it is certain that it does not hibernate, but is abroad night after night the whole year round. Indeed, as often as not, the female produces her young in the depth of winter, and indefatigable forager though she is, must often be sore pressed to provide food for her litter. At times conditions are too severe, and a tragedy ensues. At Mullyon, in Mount's Bay, one bitterly cold December, when the Poldhu stream was frozen and the sea too rough and discoloured for the otter to fish, the poor creature in her extremity crept into a bungalow in the course of erection, and was there found curled up dead.

It seems to me a matter for regret that such an interesting beast is not better known; and the present narrative is an attempt to portray it amidst the wild surroundings that are so congenial to its shy nature.

The critical reader will perhaps wonder at the daring that essays to interpret the workings of the most subtle of animal brains, but I submit that the inferences are, for the most part, of a very safe character; and modest as they are, they would not have been adventured on, had it not been for my long familiarity with the ways and habits of a creature that is by general consent the most mysterious and inscrutable of our fauna, for the incidents described embody the gleanings of a lifetime of observation and inquiry. It will be noted that I agree with those who hold that in pursuit of fish the otter is guided wholly by sight, though it may well be that the extraordinary powers of scent which enable the creature to detect the presence of fish in a stream or pond by sniffing the surface are called into play during immersion.

The story of the otter is, I believe, now told at any length for the first time; and my hope is to bring about a wider and deeper interest in the animal, and be the means of removing some of the prejudice which unjustly attaches to it.

J.C. Tregarthen
Tregonebris
Sancreed
West Cornwall
10 March 1909

ABOUT THE AUTHOR

John Coulson Tregarthen (1855–1933) was born in Penzance, part of a family from the Scilly Isles where 'Tregarthens' is still a well-known hotel on St Mary's. He gained an honours degree in Mathematics at London University in 1878 and went on to teach mathematics at Trinity School, Stratford-upon-Avon. Within a matter of years, he had bought the school and made such a success of it that, in his late forties, he was able to sell it to the popular romantic novelist, Marie Corelli, and retire with his wife to Cornwall, to the Land's End he knew and loved so well. Over six feet tall, 'upright as a bolt and of a ruddy countenance', he was a remarkably gifted field naturalist.

Encouraged by Marie Corelli, Tregarthen began writing, and she recommended him to her publisher, John Murray. Thus began his very successful career as an author.

In 1928, he became a Bard of the Cornish Gorseth, taking as his bardic name *Mylgarer* (Lover of Wild Animals). By now he had become the acclaimed author of a number of best-selling books chronicling the life of animals including the fox, hare and badger. His animal biographies are rooted in his native Penwith and they captured the character of the beasts, portraying their lives in emotional terms (that is, in terms of an otter's or fox's life having 'ups and downs', joys and sorrows). Far from sentimental, his tales invariably involve death and, quite often and unashamedly, death at the hands of a hunt. Far from an apologist for hunting, he acknowledged that the instinct to hunt is one that we, being human animals, have to deal with in ourselves. He understood that, for the hunter to comprehend the consequences of hunting, he (or the otter or badger) needs to understand what it is to be hunted.

His writing is rightly admired for a detailed and acutely observed depiction of landscape and his finely tuned ear for Cornish dialect. Tregarthen died in 1933. He had fought to secure the dignity and freedom of nature, whether on the moors and clifftops or in the hearts of Cornish people.

This introduction to the life and work of the author is an edited and abridged version of Bert Biscoe's 'Introduction' to Tregarthen's novel, John Penrose – A Romance of the Land's End, *also published by Cornwall Editions Limited.*

AN APPRECIATION
OF J.C. TREGARTHEN

By C.C. VYVYAN

Clara Vyvyan was born in 1888 in Australia of a Cornish mother. Resident in Cornwall from the age of two, in 1929 she married Sir Courtenay Vyvyan, tenth baronet of Trelowarren. A respected writer, she was the author of many books of travel and autobiography. She died in 1975.

The measuring rod that we use in our own backyard and parlour is ill-adapted for surveying national, international or cosmic boundaries, and we Cornishmen who are now setting out to cry up our own goods must beware of falling into the snare that entraps certain minor European nations and a few addicts of regional literature.

Enamoured, like Narcissus, of their own features, confined physically by Destiny and mentally by choice within a narrow area, these introverts have one thing in common, a habit of inflating their own pygmies in season and out of season, on platform and in print, until the world might think that every Denmark has today its own Aristotle and every Switzerland its Shakespeare. Unfortunately, these pygmies never, like that commendable frog in the fable, achieve bursting point, but continue to hop and blow round their own small arena enclosed and shadowed by a chorus of admirers who stand by to administer encouragement and

praise. Heaven guard our Editor, and us his satellites, from enac-
ting such a scene in our own backyard that is set between Land's
End and Tamar!

In assessing their own local writers, patriots sometimes forget
that these cannot attain the first rank unless they transcend their
individual country, as Hardy transcended Wessex and Mistral
Provence and W.H. Hudson the Pampas and Arabian Lawrence
the desert and Cervantes La Mancha, by setting their local outlook
and experience against a background of that unknown space and
time which some call the fourth dimension and others call eter-
nity. What should they know of Cornwall who only Cornwall
know? Bearing these things in mind, we shall be wise enough to
refrain from making extravagant claims for Cornish celebrities.

All this is written as a warning to myself before I begin to
voice my admiration for the writings of J.C. Tregarthen.

The small peninsula in which, for so many years, he lived and
worked and studied the habits of wild animals, gave him all the
material that he needed; moreover, so intimately did he sense, so
artlessly portray the almost mystic union between those living
animals of the countryside and the very stones among which they
wander, the earth that they tread and the sea whose dirge is their
daily companion, that it would not be possible to separate in
thought those creatures of a day from their immemorial haunts.
He voices all this in the preface to *Wild Life at the Land's End*.
'These surviving mammals,' he says, 'add to the attractions of a
coast and countryside over which broods the silence of a mysterious past. The fascination which these creatures have for me dates
from boyhood, when I once caught a glimpse of a badger stealing
over a cairn in the grey of early dawn.'

There is no need to make extravagant claims for Tregarthen in the matter of style, dramatic talent or originality. His range was narrow, not only in the actual mileage that he covered before he wrote his animal biographies but also in his gifts and capabilities as a writer; he had, however, three quiet virtues that give a certain fine quality to his work, these virtues being better equipment for a writer on natural history than any mere mastery of high-sounding words, any far-flung wealth of material. He was selfless, careful and sensitive to unseen things. Thus it was that he acquired direct contact with his subject, and in the end was able to project himself into the very soul of the otter, the badger, the hare, the fox, the seal. At times he is able to suppress himself completely as a medium, and we do not feel that he is holding the mirror up to Nature, for he is presenting what he has seen and felt in such simple fashion that we look through his writing, as we might look through a pane of glass, at the growth, movements, activities, loves, fears and encounters of his intimate wild friends.

Such writing does not lend itself to quotation, for his constant awareness of the sharpened senses of nocturnal animals, of their powers of light movement, scent, hearing, is spread out through all his narrative. Now and then, however, a quite simple phrase or two will convey this awareness to us as we read; as, for example, the description of the badger cubs emerging for the first time from their earth.

> They were nine weeks old when she called to the cubs to follow, and allowed them their first view of the upper world. It was a beautiful June night and as peaceful as it was beautiful. Brock and his sister, who had frisked and frolicked whilst in the tunnel, were taken aback at the sight that met their eyes. Instead of the den, with its low,

unlighted roof, there was a vast sky far away, full of
stars; instead of their short length of tunnel for romps,
a limitless playground lay outspread at their feet, and a
fresh breeze struck cool on them after the close atmosphere of the sett.

Carefully and without haste he adds one detail to another and
each has been gained by patient observation, each is recorded with
fidelity to the background; you penetrate with the writer to the air-
less, rock-bound earth of the badger, you smell the bitter scent of
the iris leaf on the otter's lake, you see the shadow of the ash tree on
the pool at midnight and the water all about that shadow shining
like quicksilver, you begin to prick you ears and sniff the air,
glancing quickly to right and left, almost you become endowed with
animal senses as you read his stories of the hunted fox or hare or
otter, of the digging out of the white badger.

Building from without inwards, you may say. How can you
achieve a living picture by adding one dry fact to another? Is a mere
observer ever a creator? Well, without within, within without, it is
all a never-ending circle. The fact remains that Tregarthen's
animals are not still-life pictures; they are alive and yet we know
that the mere addition of touch to touch in paint, in words, in
modelling, can never be creative work. Art demands always something more; the Something More that creeps between the words of
a poem, between the lines of a drawing, that dwells triumphantly
in music. What is it? Passion, I should say, or rather the reflection
of passion, for the mere brain, with all its range and power, never
can produce a work of art that touches down to the quick of
another person's being. Akin to the rainbow illumined by the
passion of a storm, to the seed impelled by the life urge to thrust

up through dark earth and burst asunder into leaf and blossom, to the wave charging blindly across oceans to hurl itself on rock, all artists are impelled or informed by some passionate force greater than themselves. Such a force no doubt impelled this quiet schoolmaster to forgo sleep, leisure, comfort, in his night-and-day study of wild animals.

Such a force could hardly expend itself and die away into flatness. No; as we read we no longer see his animals with the eyes of a human onlooker. We become, for the time being, those animals themselves.

With the Jack hare of Bartinney, we race away from the grey-hounds, jumping the gate as the hounds pass underneath, doubling, leaping, circling over that wild moorland country; with the otter we travel from stream to pond and moorland, and down again to cliff or estuary, we haunt morasses, caverns, tree-roots and ancient travel-ways across country that leads from one stream to another, we lie up when the sun appears and steal out again when dusk can hide our movements.

Now and then this writer will credit animals with the power of visualizing memory and even of human speech. The otter cubs, for instance, lay awake 'thinking of an incident of the night'; it was not the croaking of the frogs nor the trail across the yard that occupied their thoughts but the miller looking out from his bed-room, 'the night-capped monster whom they still pictured as he appeared at the window'.

This tendency may be noted also in the fox biography which is written throughout in the first person; his mother the vixen, his wife the younger vixen, the badger whose sett he inhabits, the earth-stopper and the farmer who take him captive, and even the strange fox who arrives from the Black Forest, all converse in human speech which is understood and recorded by the hero fox.

The reader is brought up with a jerk, it is as if the author, like certain writers and broadcasters, were 'talking down' to the children. So many animal writers fall into this habit sooner or later, and Tregarthen is, on the whole, remarkably free from it.

There are moments when the reader may feel that these animal stories are rather flat; they lead us on through night after night of movement, gambolling, mating, foraging. Sooner or later, however, there will be a crisis and a quickening of the pace. A man will cross the path of our nocturnal animal; a cruel winter will curtail his food supplies; or a flood will threaten to drown him in his lair. There is the story of the great coursing match when rival greyhounds pursue the hare, of the otter hunt, of digging out the white badger. There are also the death scenes which must find a place in any complete biography, and here, or so it seems to me, Tregarthen writes in the true classic style; he does not strut nor posture nor exclaim to express his own inner knowledge of the situation, but he does not sentimentalize about the troubles of his well-beloved animals. In the Homeric tradition, he narrates simply and objectively each phase of any final tragedy, leaving the sadness or the horror to speak for itself. Quietly and truthfully he tells of the death of the female badger in a trap, breaking her teeth on the iron as she tries to free her nearly severed foot, trying to dig herself into the ground, trap and all. Briefly and without comment he narrates the end of the exciting story of the otter hunt:

> The hounds were nearly exhausted as he, and though
> they gained on him, it was not until they came to the
> calm water beyond the breaking wave that they
> managed to hold him and worry his life out.

Study of Tregarthen's books may lead to a conviction that he drew an almost mystic power from the West-country stretch of land that he knew and loved so well. When he takes, instead of animals, human beings for his heroes, he is less sure of himself and less convincing; except when he draws the memorable figure of Andrew, the old earth-stopper. *John Penrose*, it is true, is alive and his life story goes forward with a swing and a rhythm that holds the reader, but then John himself never left the land, and indeed not only his movements and adventures but all his thoughts were centred in the land on which he worked as his father had worked before him.

In *The Smuggler's Daughter*, which takes us among riding and preventive officers and smugglers, he seems to have lost the power of making his figures live; in fact, some of them behave like sticks or automaton, and the freshness and charm of John Penrose as a lover is a strange contrast to the perfunctory courtship of Marston.

In both these works of fiction, however, as in his animal biographies, his local colour is impeccable, whether laid on in broad sweeps or, with the lightest touch. Dialect, landmarks, locality of field, river, cairn and cromlech, each and all were clear to him as the veins in his own hand. We have Mr Thomas Bolitho in his bank, shrewd and kindly; and the much-travelled pedlar who had seen St Paul's Cathedral so often that he never could see the dome of Penzance market-place without thinking of it; Sir Rose, the autocratic squire with his passion for sport; the old woman recalling Wesley pausing in his August sermon to hear a grey-bird sing, and Richard Pentreath, her listener, saying to himself that grey-birds do not sing in August.

All through his works this feeling for the country sounds, sometimes like a loud chorus, sometimes like a faint echo. Myself,

I like the echoes best; here is one from *The Smuggler's Daughter*, on mortgaged land:

> Do you know there are farms in this parish dipped so deep that all that's left to the owner is the wind that blows over them. And semmin' to me neither the tenant nor the hosses work with the same spirit when they get to know it.

Yes, we can claim with conviction that Tregarthen is in the direct line of descent from the great naturalist writers. Audubon may range over the spaces of America, and Hudson from Patagonia to Land's End and the Wiltshire downs, and Richard Jefferies through the southern counties, and William Beebe in the swamps of Florida that are neither land nor sea, but Tregarthen will seldom stir from one small corner of one small county of our little island.

He went about his self-appointed task with seeing eyes, selfless, sincere and faithful.

The Publishers wish to thank Donald Rawe and Bert Biscoe for drawing attention to this article, which first appeared in The Cornish Review, *no 4, 1950.*

'THE COMEBACK KID'

By HOWARD CURNOW

Howard Curnow is from an old Cornish farming family and has a long-felt, intimate contact with the Cornish countryside. On returning to live in Cornwall in the 1970s he joined the Cornwall Wildlife Trust, largely because of his increasing concern over the losses to 'Wild Cornwall' caused by modern farming practices and the inexorable march of concrete and tarmac.

Despite the continuing huge losses, his involvement with CWT during this time has engendered in him no small degree of pride and satisfaction that without the work done by the Trust in the past 40 years Cornwall would today be a poorer place in which to live. A good example of this is the gallant recovery of the otter, after being near to extinction. This alone is in no small part a tribute to the Wildlife Trust of Cornwall, of which Howard became Chairman five years ago.

John Coulson Tregarthen was without doubt one of the greats amongst the great Cornishmen of the 19th and 20th centuries. One of the first bards of the revived Cornish Gorseth, President of the Royal Institution of Cornwall, Fellow of the Zoological Society, Justice of the Peace, mathematician and novelist, J.C. really came into his own in the field of natural history. His love of wild animals is reflected in both *The Life Story of an Otter* and in his bardic title, *Mylgarer*.

I have enjoyed two very tenuous links with this great Cornishman. I used to enjoy many a tipple with his nephew, Walter Bruce Coulson Tregarthen, and I have boasted right across the United States that San Francisco would not be the place it is without its magnificent carillion of bells in Grace Cathedral, which peal out across the city every day, the gift of Nathaniel Coulson of Penzance.

Almost certainly the inspiration for Henry Williamson's classic work, *Tarka the Otter*, written in an amazingly similar vein in 1927, was Tregarthen's *The Life Story of an Otter*, which first came out in 1909 and set dramatic new parameters for wildlife writing.

That he spent many years and countless hours meticulously observing every aspect of nature is conveyed in the beautiful prose of this book. Tregarthen takes his reader on an unsentimental study of a family of otters through the cycle from birth, to maturity, to death. The minute detail with which he describes the topography of the landscape, the changes of the seasons, the intimate yet sensitive details of the day-to-day existence of the otters and their constant, nocturnal searching for food makes this a story that could have been written by the creatures themselves. Although written at an easy pace, the narrative is so enthralling that it is difficult to put the book down.

The (National) Wildlife Trust's *Review*, under the heading, 'highlights of 2003', has a piece on 'The Comeback Kid'. They are referring to the otter, *Lutra lutra*. Why should the article be so called? Because only 30 years ago the otter was close to extinction.

Over the centuries hunting had never seriously threatened the otter population of lowland Britain, but the post-Second World War use of organo-chlorines in sheep dips, cereal dressing and as an insecticide was much deadlier. Inevitably finding its way into the watercourses and thence into the creatures living in these watery environments, the poison was carried up through the food chain to the otter. This led to many otter deaths and possible, but unrecorded, adverse effects on reproduction and cub development.

This came to a head in the late 1980s when the South West Water Authority discovered levels so high in one West Cornwall river that they put up warning notices to the anglers. Organochlorines were being used in large quantities on nearby daffodil fields. These facts came to the attention of Vic Simpson and Nick Tregenza, members of Cornwall Wildlife Trust. Immediate action led to a national newspaper picking up their publicity notice and running the headline, 'Give your mother chocolates instead of daffodils for Mother's Day'. Before midday on the same day the international producer of the offending product had issued orders to have it withdrawn from sale.

It has taken 20 years for the otter to make its comeback, but today, thanks to the vigilance of the Wildlife Trusts and their many otter-spotters, and in particular the efforts of Kate Stokes, Water for Wildlife manager for the Cornwall Wildlife Trust, and her colleagues in other parts of lowland Britain, all working in conjunction with the Environment Agency, the otter has indeed earned the title 'The Comeback Kid'. However, we cannot be complacent, and Kate makes a plea at the end of this book for more helpers to join the Otter Group because there is still so much we need to know about this secretive animal.

Hunting is banned and organo-chlorines are banned, but humans continue to be the main predator. The number one cause of otter deaths today is road-kill. Highways Authorities are aware of the problem and culverts, underpasses or simple ledges under bridges are effective. The numbers of otters killed in this way, and the subsequent examinations by Vic Simpson, national wildlife post-mortem expert at the unique Wildlife Veterinary Investigation Centre near Truro, are at least an indication that there is today a large and healthy population, with the historically strong numbers of the south and west spreading to other parts of Britain.

Their return raises a few problems with goldfish pond owners and more seriously with commercial fisheries. Advice from the Wildlife Trusts or the Environment Agency, and protective measures around these ponds, are the way forward as we celebrate the return of this much loved, vital piece of the amazing wildlife jigsaw around us. Tregarthen observes that 'an otter is a great wanderer who not only traverses the coast, explores rivers to their source, crosses hills and even mountains and can travel fifteen miles in a night'. *Lutra lutra* is a 'flagship' species. Healthy otters tell us we have a healthy countryside.

St. Hilary, 2004

CHAPTER ONE

IN THE NURSERY

ʿ§

I T WAS IN A MORASS IN A HOLLOW of the foothills that he was littered. His mother chose this inaccessible spot for the security it promised to her helpless young. In the heart of the quagmire they would be safe, she thought, from floods and – what was still more important to her – from man. She could not find a hover quite to her liking, but in lack of a better, she chose a ledge where, in an angle of the stream that drained the bog, the bank furnished a screen from the biting wind which blew up the valley and soughed over the uplands. After enlarging the ledge into a shelf, she shaped the excavation for the nest, which she fashioned out of dead rushes and withered grasses, and which she lined with the softest products that Nature offered her – tattered reed-plumes and seed-down of the bulrush. Night after night she ransacked the waste in quest of these rare spoils, lest the rude structure should be wanting in cosiness for the cubs which, even before it was quite finished, were deposited in it.

There were only two to share her affection – the intense affection of the hunted creature for its offspring. The dread of being reft of them haunted her from their birth, but happily the mites themselves knew no fear, knew nothing but the warm, furry mother who fondled and suckled them. Whelps and dam were as one, for she seldom left them save to get food; and this she sought and devoured with feverish energy, that she might the sooner return to them. She foraged sometimes, it is true, in the morass itself; but usually she had to go to the river at the foot of the long, undulating slope, and though the inconvenience of having the fishing-ground so far away was often borne in upon her, she put up with it, and never for a moment thought of moving the cubs from the safe keeping of the bog.

Under the grey skies, the rain and the sleet of January, few more cheerless scenes could be found than the moorland and the morass within it; yet there in the hollowed bank the otter and the wee, blind, downy-coated creatures she had entrusted to the chill mercies of midwinter, lay nestled in the snuggest of hovers. And the grim season would relent at times, breaking into bright days when the sun bestowed its warmth on the cold, sodden earth. Then the morass and all the hills about it were bathed in the glow, and the swollen stream, visible over the edge of the nest, glistened like silver. Quick to accept Nature's bounty for the winterlings, the otter, when satisfied that no eye observed her, took them between her lips, carried them from the gloomy hover, and laid them on a tussock which screened her where she crouched, ready to protect them. There the cubs stretched themselves and basked with quiet content in the health-giving rays. But when the sun passed behind the clouds, they would complain at the withdrawal of the warmth, and raise their blinking eyes to the sky as if protesting to a second mother against such unfeeling treatment.

For before this they had opened their eyes – black, restless eyes, like those which kept constant watch and ward over their safety. The otter, of course, managed to get a little sleep, but it was of the lightest. At the startled note of a bird, or even the sudden rustling of the reeds when a gust shook them, her head would pop up from the grasses concealing her; and she generally made a keen inspection of the skyline and of the ground within her ken before she lay down again and snatched another forty winks. But as morning after morning passed without intrusion of aught to warrant her suspicions, her vigilance gradually relaxed; and one noon, when she was very weary from the night's foraging, she curled up and fell sound asleep at her post.

Whilst she slept, a buzzard, mewing as he quartered the ground beneath, espied the cubs, and thinking they were at his mercy, stooped to seize the easy prey. He was about to lay hold of the smaller cub when the otter, awakened by the strange cry, rose from her hiding-place and confronted him. At sight of her the bird, taken aback, thought only of escape, but the mother was bent on avenging the attempted wrong. Quick as lightning she sprang at him, and, had not the hummock given way beneath her, she must have gripped him despite the frantic down-strokes of the big wings which lifted him well beyond her second leap. Her fierce eyes and bristling hair made her terrible to behold as she stood watching the marauder's retreat, and hissing the while like a fury. Then, as if fearful that the fray had attracted attention, she took her eyes off the bird and scrutinized the approaches to the morass before removing the cubs to the nest, where she stilled their complaints by fondling them until they fell asleep and forgot their sunny couch on the grass. The incident troubled the otter so greatly that, resisting all their importunities, she never again exposed them to the risk of capture.

To break the monotony of the hover, the cubs, as their limbs grew stronger, would, in the intervals of sleep, clamber to the wide parapet of the nest and take note of the things that moved within their narrow field: of trembling grasses, of the bramble spray that moved to and fro in the current, of the reeds that nodded in the wind, and, above all, of the creatures that visited the stream to feed or quench their thirst. They watched every step taken by the snipe, every thrust of his long bill; they regarded with wonder the gay kingfisher that perched on their ledge and fished in their pool; they were moved to the keenest curiosity by the old dog-fox, who stole from the reeds to drink and set their young nostrils working with his strong scent. When sure of their footing, with pads outstretched and every webbed toe expanded they advanced to the very edge of the nest, pushed their dusky grey heads through the grassy curtain, and looked down at the eddy gurgling below, contemplating the element in which their lives would be spent and whose every change they were to know.

They resembled kittens more than any other young creatures, the difference lying in their tiny ears and shy, wild eyes. But, suggestive of fear as was their look, they were not as yet conscious of the danger besetting them, even when able to scramble up the bank and sprawl about the bog. Thither the otter led them in all weathers, and it was for this duty that she hurried back to them the instant she had done foraging. Now and again the scarcity of prey or the difficulty of securing it would detain her far into the night and sorely tax the patience of the cubs, eager for her return. In the intervals of listening they would pace round the now dishevelled nest, increasing their speed as the hours passed without sign of her. At length the shrill whistle, heard even above the storm or downpour, would reach them, and set them dancing with delight. Two furry heads and little red tongues greeted the panting mother as soon as her feet rested on the ledge, and the next instant the capering creatures followed her as she led to the gambolling-ground beyond the great reed-bed. There they frolicked to their heart's content through the hours of darkness, and even after sun-up when thick fog shrouded the morass. On reaching the nest the otter suckled them to sleep, and, lying between them and the mouth of the holt, as was her invariable custom, shielded them from cold and danger.

These were happy days for the dam, but owing to the wilfulness of the male cub they did not last long. He had taken it into his head that he was big enough to go out alone, and one night out he ventured. He was more than half-way to the reed-bed when his mother found him. This first demonstration of independence caused her little concern, but she was almost beside herself with anxiety when, two days later, he made an attempt to sally out in broad daylight, and all but succeeded in getting away. He was nearly over the bank when she pulled him back by the tail and gave him a sharp nip by way of punishment. The very next day the incor-rigible fellow got even farther away; but she discovered his absence before he had got beyond the tussocks, fetched him back, and bit him severely as she laid him down in the nest. Thus disobedience brought unhappiness into the hover, and the cub, shrinking from the mother he deemed cruel, shuffled to the inmost corner, where fibrous roots protruded from the low roof, and there licked his bruises in morose isolation.

Aware now of his rashness, the otter dared not leave the nest by day as she had occasionally done before. One noon, however, impelled by her own hunger and the cubs' piteous entreaties for food, she put aside her apprehensions and stole out, leaving them to their own devices. As quickly as her pads could carry her, she made her way down the hill along the rents that fissured the peaty ground, dived across the swollen pool in the hollow below, dashed over the sward beyond some alders, and gained the wood and the river unobserved. The river was bank-high and much discoloured, but after a long quest she came on an eel abroad in the flood. Landing under some bushes on the far side, she devoured half the fish, and then, without a moment's delay, slipped into the river and floated down with the current. At a rapid pace she rounded bend after bend, came ashore at a backwater, leapt some felled trees, and regained the bog by the same hidden ways. To her dismay she found, as she had feared, the nest deserted and cold. In great distress she set out to fetch the truants home. She followed their trail to the reed-bed, through which she dashed like a thing demented, and came upon her two cubs playing in the open as fearlessly as only tame creatures may play. On sighting their mother, the runaways, instead of slinking off guilt-stricken, rushed at the full speed of their ungainly limbs to meet her, and tried by winning antics to induce her to join in their midday romp. Gladly as she would have complied, her response was to drag them into cover, take the smaller cub in her mouth, carry it to the nest, and return for the ringleader, who squealed with rage until soundly ducked in the pool below the hover. The dark-pelted creature was a conspicuous object as she splashed across the exposed spaces; but, as good fortune would have it, both she and the cubs escaped the observation of the keeper who was occasionally to be seen on the hills overlooking the morass. Still, the poor outlaw had been taught a sharp lesson, and resolved never again on any pretext to leave the cubs by day. So greatly was she perturbed by their escapade that she even longed for the moment when fear should awaken in them and whisper its monitions.

Meanwhile, she looked forward with impatience to the night when they would be able to follow her afield and learn the many lessons she was anxious to teach them; and in order to hasten the time, she devoted every hour she could spare to sharing their frolics, so that they might develop rapidly.

CHAPTER TWO

EARLY TRAINING

ᴡᴇ

W HEN THE CUBS WERE A LITTLE over eight weeks old, their mother resolved to take them to the pool and teach them to swim; so one starry night at setting-out time she led the young creatures – overjoyed, as their excited antics showed, at this new departure – to the brow of the rising ground, till then the boundary of their narrow world. There, whilst the otter stood and reconnoitred, the eyes of the cubs wandered wonderingly from slope and rushy hollow to the woods across the ravine, where a vixen was squalling. As no danger threatened, dam and whelps made for the faintly silvered pool lying so still and silent in contrast with the river that ran brawling along its boulder-strewn channel. On reaching it the mother swam slowly out, turning her head the while as if to invite the cubs to follow her, landed on the islet and, in order to work on their feelings and draw them across the water, hid herself amongst the withered sedge. This was not without its effect, as the cries of the cubs showed; yet, distressed though they were at the separation, they were afraid to commit themselves to the pool and try to join her. Thereupon the otter swam back to within a few feet of the foreland where the shrinking creatures stood and, wheeling slowly, returned again to the islet, calling as she went.

This she did many times, employing every wile she knew to coax them after her; but all in vain. For three nights, despite all her pains, she failed to tempt them beyond the shallows. At last, just when she was about to put them out of their depth, the smaller cub overcame its hesitation, waded till it lost foothold, then swam bravely across, landed with a little wriggling jump, and sent the spray flying from every silky hair along the fourteen inches of its length, as it shook itself before rolling on the sedge to dry its coat more thoroughly. The male cub, who had watched her every movement, was now beside himself at being left alone, and after running for some time up and down the bank, uttering the most piteous plaints, followed the others across and dried his fur as his sister had done. Presently they all swam back to the foreland. Before returning to the hover, they crossed and recrossed four times more; and once even, in the absence of the otter, who was away foraging, the cubs crossed alone.

From this night their fear of the water abated, and soon, with scarce a ripple to mark their smooth progress, they were able to accompany their proud mother in her circlings round and round the pool. When the smaller cub tired, the otter slackened her pace, sank very low, took it on her back, and carried it to the shallows; but the male cub always had to take care of himself. The subsequent improvement was very rapid, and at the end of a week so fond did they become of the water that when released from the hover they scurried to the pool in advance of their mother, stumbling and falling as they ran in their eagerness to reach it.

Being full of the young creature's love of 'hide-and-seek', they often concealed themselves before she came up. On hearing her approach, they drew their heads beneath the surface until only their nostrils showed and, though thrilling with excitement, kept as motionless as the alder snags about them until discovered. Then mother and cubs joined in play, disporting themselves at times on the surface, but more often in the depths. Presently they would rise, locked together as if in deadly struggle, and roll over and over like a water-logged ball in a current. All at once, and frequently whilst immersed, they would break up, land, and make the circuit of the banks, passing one another as though they were utter strangers, and then suddenly, as if by signal, take to the water again and resume their mimic warfare. Once whilst they were thus engaged the whistle of an otter reached them from the river. In a twinkling they stayed their gambols, and, floating side by side, listened until the call grew faint as the traveller passed up the valley; then they fell again to their romps.

Wonderful ease and grace marked their movements in the pool, and still more in the streams and eddies of the river, to which the otter lost no time in taking them. They spent hours shooting the rapids below the salmon pool, landing at the end of the long run where the rush of water loses its force, and regaining the head of the current by climbing the rocky bank. So attractive did this diversion prove that but for their mother's restraint the eager creatures would have left the nest for the river long before it was safe to be abroad. Once, indeed, overborne by their importunities, she so far yielded as to lead them out before the after-glow had paled; but this concession only made them more exacting. On the morrow they would have her release them the moment the sun dipped below the crest and the shadow of the upland fell on the morass. But she turned a deaf ear to their entreaties and, when they became insubordinate and attempted to force a way past her, punished them with many sharp nips and kept them back.

She was also much troubled at this time by their refusal to eat the fish with which she had been doing her best to tempt them. It mattered not whether she offered them samlet, trout, or eel, they turned from all alike, and it seemed as if they would never be brought to touch any. Nevertheless she persisted, till one night, on the bank of the deep pool below the rapids, the male cub took a trout from her mouth, and the next night, just before dawn, his sister did the same. Their aversion to solid food once overcome, they would chatter over the new diet as if to testify to the pleasure they found in the exercise of their newly acquired taste, or even hiss angrily when their savage passions were stirred by the wriggling or quivering of the fish in their grip. They held the prey between the fore-paws, slicing off delicate morsels with their pearly teeth, and champing them fine before swallowing. Most remarkable was the way they set about eating two of the fish their mother provided for them. With the trout they began at the head, but in the case of the eel they attacked the part below the vent, leaving the upper portion untouched.

This fish diet produced a most significant change: the cubs became fierce, and at the same time fearful. No longer was any restraint needed to keep them to the nest or to the holts in the river-banks, where they occasionally lay; no longer had the mother any difficulty in getting them to obey the dawn-cry and follow whither she led. Henceforth the sense of dread lay on their lives like a shadow and deepened with their development. It was seen in their readiness to crouch or make for the water at any strange sound, in their suspicion of any strange object. A bottle left on the bank by the water-bailiff caused them to take a wide detour, and the snapping of a stick under the foot of a lumbering badger nearly frightened these noiseless movers out of their wits. Once a thunderstorm terrified them with its vivid flashes, and one day even a brilliant rainbow was a source of alarm, until their mother awoke and showed no concern.

These trifling scares were followed towards the close of March by an incident they never forgot – an incident which caused the otter even greater consternation than it caused the cubs. It happened late one afternoon. The male cub had awakened from his second sleep and, with head resting on his mother's flank, sat looking at the light fade over the wind-swept morass. During a lull an unaccountable rustling in the reeds caught his ears and brought him to his feet. The startled movement aroused his mother and sister, and in a trice all three otters were watching from behind the grass screen for a sight of the noisy intruder. The next instant they saw a fox, bedraggled almost beyond recognition, stagger from the reeds, drop from the bank to the stream, lap, raise his head and listen, lap again, then toil with bog-stained body and sodden brush up the opposite bank and pass from view. He could not have got far beyond the river, for which he seemed to be heading, before a hound came in sight, then two more, followed almost immediately by the body of the pack, which poured over the brow of the upland and streamed down a gully towards the morass. Soon they had disappeared, but whine after whine reached the otters' ears, mingled with the crashing of the brake as the pack approached the stream and swept by full in their view. Some minutes later two yapping, bog-stained terriers crossed, and then the morass resumed its wonted calm. All this the otters had watched, hissing through their bared teeth, eyes starting from their sockets, and hair bristling erect on their thick necks: even when all was quiet again a great dread still possessed them. Their feral nature had been stirred to the depths, and they listened and listened, though no sound reached them save a faint toot of the horn. Setting-out time came and went, but the otters did not stir, till at length, taking heart from the owls, who filled the wood with their wild hooting, they stole down to the river.

The otter fished, but not a moment was given to gambolling, and long ere the woodman's bantam heralded the day the scared creatures sought harbourage in the branches of a fallen pine whose top lay half immersed in the river. Hidden amidst the flotsam caught by the boughs, with the deep pool just below them, they felt safe, and at length slept as soundly as they had done in the morass.

They repaired to the same hover the next day and the day following. In their waking hours they would watch the eddying water and rising trout, and at times cast a glance at the belt of timber beyond, as if attracted by the crimson blossom of the elms. Not only did the flowering of forest tree tell of the passing of winter, but green shoots of flag and reed shyly whispered the same story, and wild daffodils in glade and dell proclaimed it. A gold-crest in the tall fir had begun laying her tiny freckled eggs; a throstle on the lone poplar by the pool sang to his mate guarding her turquoise treasures by the river's bank, while the ravens up the face of the cliff were already busy feeding their young. Day by day, as the sun grew stronger and the west wind blew, the sycamores unfolded their fresh green leaves, and soon, the woodland over, all the buds, responsive to the quickened underworld, opened to greet the spring.

At the close of a hot day, when every furry wildling had felt its coat a burden, and longed for sundown and the drinking-place, the otter, who had been gradually extending her nocturnal rambles, took the cubs three miles down the river to a point where a part of the water is diverted into a tranquil mill-stream. Along its bank she brought them to the gate leading to the mill-yard, where all three stood and listened momentarily to the croaking of the frogs in the meadow beyond. Then they slipped under the low bar, crossed the yard, skirted the house, and hurried towards the ditch from which the noise proceeded. The croaking ceased on their approach, and before the otter entered the water every frog had sought a hiding-place at the bottom. The otter had scarcely dived before she was out again with two frogs in her mouth. These she skinned and gave to the cubs. Finding the morsel toothsome, and learning that if they wanted more they must fish for themselves, they joined in the easy pursuit, and for the first time in their lives satisfied their hunger with prey of their own taking.

Finally, they quarrelled like little tigers over a frog, of which each claimed possession, and so loud a chattering did they make that the miller got out of bed and opened his window to learn the cause of the disturbance. The creak of the sash silenced and alarmed them, and the next instant they and their mother were heading for the river at their best speed. An hour later the raiders started to return home by a route that took them wide of the mill where the danger lurked, thus reaching the morass without mishap; and the otter soon fell asleep, but the cubs lay awake thinking of an incident of the night. It was not the frogs that occupied their thoughts, not the bare yard or the fearsome trail across it, but the night-capped monster whom they still pictured as he appeared at the window.

CHAPTER THREE

THE FIRST TREK

꿎

N OT A SINGLE NIGHT WAS GIVEN up to frogging after the cubs had learnt to skin their prey. Forthwith the little mother, anxious to make the best of their time, led them to the moorland waters of one of the tributary streams to teach them to fish. There she had taken her first litter for their earliest lessons, and now, as then, she made for the pool above the old two-arched bridge, which she still thought most suited for a starting-point. To reach the fishing-ground betimes, she left the morass with the first shades of night and, crossing the river near the fallen pine, struck across country towards her destination. Her path led through the woodland to a waste of furze, and this to the high moorland which the stream serves to drain. Once on the heathery tableland, otter and cubs advanced at a rapid pace, and presently hit the track to the bridge, which they followed, leaving their footprints here and there on the margin of the shrunken puddles. When nearly abreast of the Giant's Quoits, first the otter and then the cubs caught the voice of the stream. The low murmur was almost lost in the sigh of the night wind, but grew louder and louder, till soon chattering run and plashing cascade appeared in the dip below.

On reaching the pool, the otter entered the water with the cubs at her side, dived, and drove the trout to the shelter of the banks.

Thereupon the cubs, who saw where the fish had fled, fell to drawing the hovers, thrusting their flat heads into hole and crevice as far
as they could reach. But the trout had found secure recesses, and
though a few felt the lips of the otters, they could not be seized, and
all but one escaped. In the pool at the bend, however, where the
bank, hollowed though it is, affords poor shelter, three were taken.
Then the captors, two on the gravel, the other on a mid-stream
boulder, lay at full length and ate their prey, munching ravenously.
The otter seemed to have set aside her fears since reaching the
moor, for never once did she trouble to listen or even to scan the
sable waste around her. All her thoughts were for the cubs, whom
she led from pool to pool, aiding them until they began to fish for
themselves; then she stood aside and watched them. Trout after
trout they caught and devoured along the winding reaches leading to the long, sullen pool in the midst of the moor, where the
mother, elated by their success, joined merrily in their gambols,
which were kept up until past the usual hovering-time.

Day was on them when they landed and sought the most invit-
ing couches the bank offered. First the cubs wormed themselves
out of sight, then the otter; and so effectually were all three concealed amongst the rocks and heather that a kestrel, hovering
over the spot, failed to get a glimpse of their brown forms, and
flew on without a suspicion of their presence. Nevertheless, the
open bank, though it had a marshy tract on one side and a deep
pool on the other, was an insecure lodging, so that it was only
because the moorland afforded no better that they returned
thither on the morrow. After that the otter, jealous for the cubs'
safety, made some five miles downstream, where the holts
amongst the roots of withy and alder were strong and sheltered
from the rain that had rendered the upland hovers so uncom-

fortable on the second day. It is true that trout were scarce, but this mattered little to the otters, for eels, their favourite prey, were abundant. Amongst them was a very large one which, on being gripped by the male cub, coiled itself round his neck and threatened to strangle him. In this predicament the otter, after a short struggle, made for the bank and rolled amongst the fern and bramble to free himself of his antagonist. Finding this of no avail, he shifted his grip to a point nearer the head and, using the terrible force of his jaws, broke the back of the eel, and so got rid of it. This fish had been captured in the shallows, but for the most part the eels were only to be had by turning over the big stones under which they darted at sight of their pursuers. The young otters eagerly joined their mother in dislodging their prey and catching them when they bolted. The swiftness of the animals in this pursuit was amazing, and no less so the quick turning movements in which rudder and fore-paw were both brought into play. Indeed the long, lissom, tapering creatures resembled huge eels, and might have been mistaken for eels but for the bubbles which rose to the surface and marked their course.

The otters kept to this part of the stream for nearly a week – that is, until the freshet which had caused the run of eels subsided, and rendered a change of quarters necessary. They then betook themselves to the main tributary on the opposite bank, three miles above the morass; but finding that some other otters had disturbed the water in front, they pressed on, and at length came up with them where the stream winds sluggishly through a swampy bottom. Two were fishing in the stream, the rest in the marsh; but presently the whole party came into view, and as they trotted along the bank were seen to be four well-grown cubs with their dam, old and slightly grizzled. They all went on in company, but as day approached drew only the best pools, and gave up fishing altogether after striking the trail of the moorman who had forded the stream at sundown. Indeed on finding the dreaded taint of man there was quite a stir amongst them, especially amongst the cubs, who kept close alongside their mothers, and wondered where harbourage was to be found on the seemingly bare upland to which they were being led. At length the scared creatures sighted the weedy lakelet where the stream rises and, just as the rim of the sun showed gained the shelter of the reeds that fringed it.

The day proved intensely hot and still, with not a breath to ripple the surface or freshen the stifling air of the brake where the otters lay panting until dusk fell and allowed them to quench their tormenting thirst without fear of detection. Then, leaving their quarters, the two families travelled together till, after crossing two naked hills, they came to a rushy flat, lined with sour water-courses, where the trail forked, and there they parted company.

The otter was bound for the head-waters of the tributary nearest the source of the river, and soon after midnight reached the boggy gathering ground with its network of runnels and chain of pools in which she and the cubs fished until the stars began to pale. Then the hunters in single file made along the slender stream for the basin below the fall, sporting together till the sun rose over the distant sea and flooded the upland with its beams. The otter, usually observant of the first signs of dawn, seemed not to heed the golden light, even when the cubs began to grow uneasy and to shoot reproachful glances at her for keeping them abroad at so late an hour. But she needed not to be reminded of her duty. She knew they ran no risk in that untrodden spot; indeed on leaving the pool she stood on the bank to gaze across the dew-spangled waste and then at the gilded crags of Lone Tarn, before at length withdrawing to a clitter some half-mile down the stream.

There the dark recesses of the pile of rocks proved a welcome retreat to the cubs, and with the music of the waters for a lullaby they soon fell asleep. They hovered there again on the morrow; after which they continued on their journey laying up under the bank of the wide pool where the stream joins the river.

At setting-out time the otter seemed half-minded to follow the river to its source, for she kept looking towards the lone hill where it rises; but presently – the lowness of the water probably weighing with her – she decided to go downstream, summoned her cubs and trotted across the bend to the head of the long rapids, where they entered the water and drifted with the current. At dawn they sought a rabbit-burrow on the river-bank so near the woods that the cubs, who lay by the mouth of one of the holes, could hear the pigeons cooing. The retreat was safe and very dry, and would have left little to desire if the rabbits had taken no notice. But the timid creatures, thoroughly alarmed at the presence of the otters, stamped almost without intermission and prevented their uninvited guests from sleeping. At noon the otter, annoyed beyond endurance, rose and chased the rabbits along the tunnels; but this only made them worse. After that the drumming was kept up in every level, and made the visitors long for night. So at early dusk, after another raid on the persecutors, the otters slid down the bank into the water and let the stream take them along reach after reach until they were far into the wood. All the way they never ceased to scan the banks; they seemed to suspect an enemy behind every tree, but surely without sufficient cause. At one spot the green eyes of a fox watched them as they passed, otherwise they floated along unnoticed save by the bats flitting up and down the dark spaces beneath the over hanging boughs. On reaching the fallen pine they began to fish, and so continued all the way to the salmon pool, where they sported till dawn drove them again to the morass.

During the weeks that followed they kept to the neighbourhood of the old nursery, lying up for the most part under rocks and tree-roots at the water's edge, but occasionally in the morass itself. It was whilst couching there that the otter, alarmed by the continued fall of the river and the exposure of the mouths of the strongest hovers, suddenly resolved to make for the tidal waters, whose holts are unaffected by droughts, and where she could teach the cubs many new lessons. She first thought of going down the river to the estuary, but changed her plans almost at the last moment and determined to make for a creek where she had had good fishing with her mate, the father of the cubs. The destination was two good marches distant, but she knew a stronghold by the way where they could lodge, and from which they could easily reach the creek on the following night.

In her anxiety to gain this refuge before dawn, she left her couch in the reed-bed at early dusk and, full of her purpose, made for the old hover where the cubs always slept when in the morass. Hearing the faint rustle of the herbage as she approached, the quick-eared creatures left the nest, and when she came up, fell into their place at her side. Leading past the pool to the river, she crossed it and headed towards the woodman's cottage. The rapid pace at which the animals travelled soon brought them within sight of the low, thatched building beneath its sheltering oak, but as nothing stirred they passed close to the garden fence and into the gloom of the pines beyond.

A happier little band of nomads could not be found than the otter and her cubs, quite unsuspicious of danger, though they were running straight into its jaws. At a sudden turn of the mossy track where rocks contract the way they came face to face with Venom, the woodman's terrier. Venom was returning from a badgers' sett which he visited whenever he could slip away unobserved, and his begrimed and bloodstained condition told how severe had been the fray between him and one of the badgers. He looked a woebe-gone mongrel as he limped along on three legs; but the instant he found himself face to face with the strangers he forgot his fatigue and flew at the otter's throat with a fury that threatened to make short work of her. He soon discovered, however, that he had caught a Tartar. The shaking he gave her had little other result than further to exhaust himself, while the otter began punishing him about the face and shoulders, making her teeth meet at every bite. Besides inflicting severe wounds, she was actually pushing the dog back, and after a prolonged tussle was clear of the rocks and close to a fallen tree from which the terrified cubs were watching the fray. Another scrimmage here took place, even longer and fiercer than the first: then the dog hesitated to renew the fight and stood on the defensive. Thereupon the otter, whose one thought was escape, joined the cubs and made off. The sight of their retreat was, however, more than Venom could stand, and they had scarce-ly disappeared before he was in pursuit. On overtaking them, he laid hold of the male cub, probably mistaking him for his mother. With a viciousness that belied his cubhood, the young dog-otter closed with his first assailant, and would have made a brave fight had he been allowed to conduct it alone. But he was not. Like a tiger the mother fell on the terrier, and it looked as if the dog would be cut to pieces. His one thought, however, was to destroy the vermin, and instead of drawing off as he might have done at the foot of the steep slope, down which they fell rather than rolled, he actually closed again, fought to the edge of the pool there, even held on to the otter when she dived, and kept his hold until his lungs were exhausted. Then he let go, but on coming to the surface he did not make for the bank. He swam round and round, looking for his enemy, and only when he had lost hope of viewing her again did he land at last. On being freed from his grip, the otter had made her way close along the bottom to the upper end of the pool, where the cubs were waiting for her among some rushes. From their shelter mother and cubs now watched the movements of their puzzled foe, who began examining the banks of the pool. When he came near, they sank almost out of sight, their nostrils alone showing, and so remained until he had time to pass; then the otter raised her head to reconnoitre. Once she did so she found the terrier standing within a few yards, but looking so intently in another direction that he failed to sight her; whereupon she sank again as noiselessly as she had risen, not leaving even her nostrils exposed. A score of times, at least, did the dog make the circuit of the pool; and had he been able to scent the otter – a thing which but few dogs can do – he must at least have driven them from their shelter, and possibly from the pool, for it was very small. Yet, insensible though he was to the scent, he was so convinced the animals were there that, after departing, he actually came back and looked again before taking himself off for good and leaving the otters free to resume their interrupted march.

For three hours they had been detained, and now, hurry as they might, it was impossible to reach the cairn before daybreak. Indeed, they were yet two miles away when the ridges above them were touched by the risen sun. To add to their troubles a magpie espied them, and though they were strange to him as to the terrier, he knew they were nightlings with no right to be abroad after sunrise, and mobbed them as he would have mobbed a leash of foxes. Under the brambles and osmunda ferns they were hidden from the pest, but in the open he had them at his mercy and, now fluttering just beyond their reach, now hopping from branch to branch of rowan or alder or wild-cherry, he annoyed then with impunity. At last they came to the foot of the slope at the head of the ravine, threaded the furze as fast as their pads could carry them, reached the pile of rocks, and one by one disappeared through the narrow crevice near its base. The magpie, however, instead of flying off, perched on the pinnacle of the cairn and, with his head knowingly cocked on one side, watched for their reappearance. Long, long he waited, but as the creatures made no sign, he tired, took wing, flew down the ravine past the precipice where the ravens had their nest, and regained the wood of which he was so vigilant a sentinel.

The persecuted beasts soon forgot the magpie, but the terrier had left a deeper memory, and all three were long in falling asleep. The otter, indeed, was still awake at noon, when a weasel threaded the way to the heart of the cairn, and, poking his snake-like head round the angle of rock, saw the curled-up forms of the animals whose scent had drawn him thither. But a single peep satisfied his curiosity, and he went out into the blazing sunlight, fragrant with the perfume of the furze. Then the mother otter slept like the cubs.

The ravine was weird with the shades of night, raven and magpie were asleep, when the nomads left the cairn and took to the trail. Like three shadows they stole over the crest above and entered the covert. In the silence of that still, sultry night they might have been heard forcing a way where the furze was densest, and presently they emerged from the lower edge, and, traversing a strip of open ground where a rabbit was feeding, came to a stream. This they crossed by springing from rock to rock, the otter first and the male cub last. In the same order they threaded the oak coppice that clad the opposite steep, and made their way over the craggy summit that crowned it. And so they passed stream after stream, surmounted ridge after ridge of the wild watershed, and gained the outlying spur where the culti-vated lowland lay before them. It looked like a sombre, blurred plain unrelieved by water, until the moon rode clear of the clouds and revealed the winding reaches of the tidal creek for which they were bound. Their destination was yet a good way off, but as the going was now very easy the tireless creatures covered the fields at a swinging pace. The pastures seemed strange to the cubs; stranger still the sheep and cattle, asleep at such an hour without a bush to hide them; but leaving them lying there, the otters kept straight on. A homestead rose almost across their trail; the trail, however, had been traced ages before the buildings were raised or even the land was broken, and though disturbed by spade and plough a thousand times, it was still the otters' way, so mother and cubs kept to it faith-fully, past the snow-white hawthorns and into the rickyard, where they stayed to roll and dry their coats, wet from the mowing-grass. The stamping of a horse's feet sent them off before they had finished; but what alarmed them much more was a scarecrow in a top-hat standing amongst the growing corn. The suspicious creatures gave a wide berth to this horror, and kept looking back to see whether it was following, until presently they caught the scent of water; then they never gave it another thought.

In their eagerness to reach the fishing-ground they increased their pace across the three enclosures that separated them from it; but at the sight of the smooth, broad creek the cubs stood and gazed, till a call from their mother reminded them there was no time to be lost. So they made down the bank and over the beach to join her on the rocky foreland, round which the current was eddying. Together they dived and scoured the sandy bed in search of prey. In her anxiety to secure supper, the otter soon got separated from the cubs, who, through inexperience, wasted their efforts in vain pursuit of the bass instead of questing for the flat-fish that were to be had for the finding. In the end they tired without having obtained a meal. The last time they landed they were near the wooded island where the herons build, a long way from the point where they took to the tide, and it was whilst lapping the water of a runnel there that they heard their mother's call from far down the creek. At once they hurried along the strand, answering as they ran, and even after they had taken to the flood they repeated their shrill whistlings until they reached her side. To their delight, a big flat-fish lay at her feet, its white underside uppermost. The smell of the prey, strange though it was, so pleased them that their nostrils twitched with anticipation. Indeed, the flounder was an appetizing morsel for creatures sated with eels and trout, and soon all three were busy devouring it. They were not long over the feast, but they had scarcely finished when the grey light stealing across the creek drove them to a cave in the overgrown bank.

This was not a hover suddenly chanced on, but a much-frequented place of call that the otter intended making for when she left the cairn. The dank vault had been occupied the day before, as was evident from the dry place on the slab, but it was untenanted then, save by a few bats hanging from the low roof, and it afforded the new-comers the accommodation they required. The mother chose the ledge close to the landing-place, whilst the cubs scrambled to a shelf above, along the rude way worn in the slaty wall by generations of their tribe. Before curling up for the day, the otters, as was their wont, teased with their claws every bit of under-fur, and removed the thorns and furze-spines about which it had matted. Then, liking the taste of the salt water, they licked themselves until their glossy coats were as smooth as satin. As soon as their toilet was finished they settled down to sleep, and so soft was their breathing, so thoroughly did their dark pelt harmonize with its surroundings, that there was nothing to betray their presence except eyes which glowed in the sombre light until the lids closed and hid their amber fires.

CHAPTER FOUR

AT THE CREEK

ᵍ

T HE OTTER WAS AWAKENED about noon by the patter and drip of the rain that had silenced the birds in the woods outside, but the cubs slept through it all. The downpour, which lasted off and on for hours, ceased towards sundown, and at star-peep the sky had cleared of clouds, save where a black pall hung over the uplands. The otters then stole from the cave, coming singly through the mouth and, keeping within the shadow of the rocky wall, landed on the beach beyond.

After shaking their coats, they made down the creek over the rain-pitted sand until nearly abreast of a rock showing above the surface, and there took to the water. For awhile it looked as if they meant to cross to the opposite shore, but on reaching midstream they dived, and the next minute were busy detaching mussels from the bed of the channel. The bubbles which kept rising showed the position of the animals, which presently came up with their mouths full of shell-fish and swam swiftly to land. There the otter dropped the mussels she carried, seized one between her paws, bit off the end of the shell and devoured the fish. Scarcely had she swallowed it before the cubs were busy breaking the brittle shells and feasting on the succulent contents; and the crackling noise that broke the silence would have puzzled any chance visitor to the wood, but was no unfamiliar sound to the birds that roosted in the overhanging oaks. The otters made several journeys to and from the mussel-bed, till they had eaten their fill; then fell to gambolling on the edge of the tideway, to the annoyance of a heron, which soon took wing for a station higher up the creek. Two or three hours they there spent in play, varied by excursions into the wood, where they startled a hare and put the brooding pheasants in a fever. Once they penetrated to the craggy summit, climbed the rocks, lapped the water in the highest of the basins, and, before jumping down, gazed across the intervening country to where the estuary glimmered between its dusky shores.

The beach was almost covered by the advancing tide when the otters took to the water and drifted up with the flood. Their outstretched limbs being flush with the surface, they looked like floating skins as the current bore them along; but soon after passing the heron, spectral in the uncertain light, they began swimming, and so entered the cave, where they shook their coats and lay down in the places they had occupied the day before. The lapping of the tide was their slumber-song, and the happy creatures were sound asleep before the last of the bats came flitting in to roost.

That day a fiery sun beat down upon the country-side and exhausted toiler and sportsman abroad in the sweltering heat. The mower sweated and panted behind the scythe, the otter-hunters crossing the moor longed for the cool woods they had left, and the boy on the smack at the end of the creek gobbled up his pasty to spend the dinner-hour in the pool beneath the bridge. Not only man and boy suffered from the heat; beast and bird too sought the shade, abandoning their haunts to the insect hosts that revelled in the scorching rays. The flower-gay selvage margining the far shore of the creek and the tangle of honey-suckle and wild-rose that curtained the portals of the otters' lair, hummed with the noise of countless wings. Honey-bees were there, green-bodied flies and blue, and, preying on them, dragon-flies that darted to and fro, casting sharp shadows on yellow sand-bank and sapphire pool. But, glaring and dazzling as was the light, no ray penetrated the gloom that shrouded the otters, who never moved until near their usual stirring-time. Then they rose, but only to stretch themselves, for they lay down again, listened to the fading voices of the mowers, and watched the afterglow pale upon the face of the water.

At length, when all was still and the light sombre, they slipped noiselessly into the current, raising scarce a ripple as they passed from pool to pool on their way down the creek. They landed at the turn below the mussel-bed to quench their thirst, then took to the water again, and were soon busy disporting themselves in Deadman's Pool. On leaving it, they moved forward, climbing every rock, and resting there as if they enjoyed the warmth till, two miles beyond the pool, they came to where the creek broadens between marshy flats given over to wild-fowl. As it was in this reach that the otter intended to hunt when the coming tide had brought up the fish that came there to feed, she and the cubs landed and played about on the bank to while away the time of waiting. Presently they entered the fen, where they disturbed some wild-duck and set the moorhens calling in notes of alarm which were taken up by the fowl on the other side of the creek, but subsided the instant the intruders' gambols showed they had no murderous intentions.

Close on midnight, when the tide was about half flood, the otter, with the cubs at her side, re-entered the creek in search of flat-fish. Her quest was no easy one, for she had crossed the sandy bottom but once before the fish, becoming aware of the presence of their dreaded enemies, gave up feeding, and buried themselves in the sand. A pair of eyes dotted here and there about the wide bed was all that showed, and it was for this sign of the fish's presence that the otter searched, jerking her head this way and that to scan the ground on each side of her course. At the fourth dive she suddenly sighted prey, as suddenly ceased propelling herself, and stopped within a foot of the spot where the restless eyes were watching her, while the cubs, who had shot past, turned, full of wonder, and rejoined their mother. Then the otter stretched out a fore-leg, touched the plaice through the thin layer of sand and put it to flight. The cubs, taken aback by the unexpected appearance of the fish, did not move till it had got some yards away, but once in pursuit the male cub soon recovered the lost ground, seized the prey, rose to the surface, and swam ashore. Two more plaice were captured within the hour, one by the cubs without assistance, and from that moment their mother let them quarter the sand alone. They propelled themselves by their hind-legs as their mother did, the fore-legs being pressed against the side, except when used for sudden turning movements; but on rising to the surface all four limbs came into play, while the massive tail alone did the steering. When their hunger was appeased they made up the creek, ducking their heads as they went, until a stone fell from the crumbling cliff above Deadman's Pool and scared them; they then gave over their bobbing, but redoubled their speed, passing the flotsam at a rapid pace, and all the way to the cave they scanned the banks as if they dreaded an ambush, though they had never once been waylaid.

That day, whilst awaiting the dusk, the otter resolved to make a journey up the creek after the school bass. The tide did not serve before midnight; then the rain, which had threatened, began to fall and, as the animals drifted by the herons' island, was coming down in torrents, but under it the current bore them rapidly along the reaches without sign of man's neighbourhood, save a disused limekiln, until the last bend brought them within sight of a bridge and of the hamlet that straggles down the hillside to a wharf on the water's edge. When they were abreast of it the bass began to rise, and drew them in pursuit. Shooting up from below, the hunters seized the unsuspecting fish, and soon were busy eating their take, the cubs on the buoys, the otter on a projecting stone of one of the buttresses of the bridge. Once all three landed under the farthest arch and dropped their prey in affright at the unexpected presence of the parish constable, who was sheltering there and was almost as much scared himself.

Soon the crowing of the village cocks warned the otter that she ought to withdraw; but it was not until the smoke began to rise from the galley of the smack by the wharf that she at last gave up fishing and made for the drain hard by, where she had twice laid up before. Against a strong head of water they forced their way up the tunnel till they came to the rude ledges of masonry in it, and there curled up as best they could for the day. The cubs had never hovered in such scant quarters before, but their discomfort was as nothing in comparison with the terror which the rumbling of a van over their heads occasioned them. In the course of the morning, towards noon, things were still worse. A sheepdog with a nose for otters winded them, and came and sniffed at the grating within a couple of yards of where they lay. In his excitement he kept pawing the iron bars and whimpering until the cry of 'Shep, boy!' recalled him to the flock, the patter of whose feet had set the

otters on the alert before the dog darkened the twilight of their
hiding-place. These were the great alarms of the day – indeed, the
only alarms, for the otters took little notice of the bell which rang
each time a customer entered the grocer's shop, and scarcely more
of the voices of the children abroad when the rain ceased.

The street was deserted and the windows aglow when the
otters made their way down the drain and, after listening at the
mouth, stole out into the moonlight. They ran some danger of
being seen as they approached the smack, and again after passing
it, but fortune favoured them; they escaped observation, and got
clear away.

They kept to the margin of the creek till near the limekiln.
Then the otter struck inland, with stealthy motion threading the
tufts that covered the rising ground. Half-way up the slope she
suddenly turned and looked at the cubs as if a careless step had
annoyed her, but at once resumed her stalk. Presently her nostrils
twitched; she had scented a rabbit that was feeding just over the
brow. Coming within sight of the unsuspecting creature she gathered herself for a spring, and a fox could scarcely have launched
itself more swiftly than did the otter. A timely movement, however, saved the rabbit, which, with others feeding there, gained the
shelter of the bank. Balked of her prey, the otter stood for a
moment where the unavailing leap had taken her, but as soon as
the cubs came up she made for the biggest of the holes, and
through it all three disappeared. Rabbits popping out here and
there along the bank showed how quickly the otters traversed the
set, and presently the male cub, looking with its arched back like a
big ferret, issued from the hole out of which a rabbit had come
and, following the scent with great eagerness, entered another hole
into which it had darted. The mother otter, meanwhile, had been

more successful, for a squeal underground heralded her appearance with a dead rabbit in her mouth, closely followed by the cubs. When she had bitten off the head and the pads, she removed the skin as if it had been a glove, and broke up the carcass. Except for a few moorhen, it was the first warm prey the cubs had eaten, and they devoured it greedily, as they did their share of another rabbit surprised in the furze beyond the burrow. This ended the night's hunting, and leaving the out-turned skins on the turf, the otters went back to the creek across the dewy grass which they marked with a clearly visible track.

On gaining the shore they burst into a gallop from sheer high spirits, spurning the sand as they hurried along the lone reach in a silence unbroken save by the sob of the restless tide that was mounting along their path. Within a mile of the heronry they crossed the flood and sported in the great eddy there; at times they landed on the cone-shaped rock that rose amidst the swirl and cast its inky shadow on the silvery surface. The playful creatures seemed to have set aside their fears and lingered till sunrise, when the shout of a farm-boy to a neighbour caused them to dive and make for the cave. Time after time they rose to breathe, always in the slack water, and at last, when the brimming tide was all ablush and every songster pouring out its greetings to the sun, they gained their sanctuary beyond the reach of danger.

Thus day followed day and week succeeded week, until they had got to know the creek as they knew the morass. By the beginning of August there was not an inlet left unexplored nor a stream unvisited. The biggest of the streams they followed to its source among the hills, within easy reach of the sea, and laid up there, but partly retraced their steps the next night, and curled up at dawn beneath the roots of a sycamore that overhung a mill-pool. That day very heavy rain fell, and continued till a late hour, soaking the country-side and causing even the cave to drip, to the discomfort of the otters, who repaired there on the morrow. This decided the otter to make without further delay for the sea, and that night, after a big feast on the mussels, she led the cubs along the widening reaches to the estuary and couched on an island at the meeting of the waters. A barge drifted by at sunrise; later a peel leaped within a few feet of them; but the otters heeded neither the one nor the other, nor, indeed, did they raise their heads until a boy, blowing a penny may-horn, came to fetch the geese from the moor opposite, and startled them not a little. But by this time the sun was dipping below the pines near the homestead; it was almost time to be afoot, and as soon as the stars were bright, the otters took to the water and began the descent of the estuary.

The river, in spate after the rains, bore them swiftly along, now between long spits of sand, now close to the shadowed banks, dotted here and there with glow-worms. The surroundings were as peaceful as the drifting was easy; yet safe as the way seemed there was danger ahead, and a mile or so down they came on one of the worst enemies of their kind. They saw him the instant they rounded the bend; and little wonder, for the burly figure was clearly outlined against the latticed window of the keeper's cottage. Had he moved, they would merely have sunk out of sight; had he coughed or sneezed, they would have dived, to reappear a furlong below. But to scare them was the last thing he wished, and, excited though he was, he never moved a muscle. He had set a trap for the otters, which he knew would follow the peel; and since dusk he had been all ears for the rattle of the chain that would tell of a capture. As soon as they were gone by, he rose and tiptoed along the bank, wondering, as he picked his way, what made them go down when the peel were running. By the trunk of a dead ash he stopped to listen.

The otters, on coming to the loop where the estuary wellnigh returns upon itself, landed, as the keeper knew they would, and passed through a belt of young larch to a glade in which the still air was heavy with the scent of flower and fern, and a night-jar was busy among the moths. When nearly across it, the otter swerved from the trail to avoid the coppice where her mate had been trapped. It was not likely she could mistake the spot, for she had stood by him till at dawn the footfall of the keeper had driven her away. She had even returned the two following nights, and called and called and called before going off alone to prepare a nest for her unborn cubs. And now another trouble beset her: the male cub persisted in following the trail, and owing to his great strength, succeeded, despite all her efforts, in getting amongst the bushes where the trap was set. He was on the point of putting his pad on the plate, when, in desperation, she bit him and made him turn. As he did so she closed with him, for she would rather kill him than suffer him to fall a victim to man; but when, at the sound of the struggle, the keeper came crashing through the under-growth, the otter made off, and the cub followed her.

They struck the estuary near a jetty piled with bundles of oak-bark, floundered through the mud, and reached the river. The tedious bend, of which the otters had crossed the neck, now lay behind, and in front stretched the long reach marked by broad sand-banks that the tide was beginning to crawl over. So otter and cubs, after passing two branch creeks, musical with the whistlings of night-feeding birds, came to the deeper water, where hulks rode at their last anchorage, and, farther on, to the landlocked haven in which tall-masted vessels swung to their moorings, and the lights of a little seaport and fishing village winked at one another across the salt waters. On viewing the uncanny lights and hearing the shouts of a drunken sailor the male cub sidled up to his mother; and great was his relief when she rounded the rocky promontory that projects into the harbour, and entered the tranquil creek, whose waters reflected only the friendly moon.

CHAPTER FIVE

SEA AND MARSH

HE OTTERS LANDED OPPOSITE a white buoy, and, to pass
the time till the fish came in, played about on the rocks
that strewed the shore. When the tide had covered
most of them, the otter set out to reconnoitre, and had not been
gone long before she summoned the cubs to join her. At the
signal they took to the water, and soon reached the spot where she
awaited them. On seeing her excitement they became excited too,
dived the instant she did, and the three, swimming in line abreast,
soon viewed the prey. It was but the merest glimpse they got of
half a score tails, for the fish, finding there were three otters,
wheeled round in affright and fled before their advance. At this
timid manoeuvre, so favourable to their purpose, the otters, eager
though they were to seize the prey, rose to vent, and on resuming
the chase came on the alarmed mullet in a fathom of water.
Further retreat meant certain capture, and the mullet – craftiest of
all the finny tribe – knew it. So the little school of fish made a dash
for the deeper water, and, as the otters flashed up from beneath to
seize them, scattered, leaping wildly to avoid the fatal grip. The
confusion of that moment taxes description, but one detail stands
out clear – the effort of the otter to reach the leader in its leap for
life. She did indeed lip it, but no more; and the fish, which in its fall
splashed the water into ripples of silver, got right away and

resumed the lead of the retreating shoal. A few scales only remained to mark the scene of the fray, and the chagrin of the otters was complete when, on drawing the rest of the water blank, they realized that every mullet had escaped.

The disappointed hunters landed through the maggoty seaweed which had attracted the fish, and making their way along the stream that flows into the creek, reached the mill where the otter intended to hover. To her dismay she found the holt behind the wheel in possession of another otter with cubs, and quite young ones, as she could tell by their squeals. It was a difficult situation, for day was near; but she was equal to it. Without losing an instant, she hastened back along her trail towards the only other lodging she knew within easy reach – a hole in the wall of the quay. They might be detected whilst making for it, so the mother scanned the sleeping port from the end of the promontory before committing herself to the open; but as nobody stirred, the three made across the estuary straight towards it. When they were about mid-passage, where the tide ran strongest, a big fish leaped clear of the water and fell with a resounding splash. It was a salmon. The cubs turned their questioning eyes on their mother, but she gave no heed. She was filled with anxiety lest the hole in the quay should prove to be beyond their reach. High above the water though it was, she herself entered it easily, for she could throw herself out of the water almost like a seal; but, as she had feared, the cubs fell back again and again. The whistling of the distressed creatures must have been audible to anyone on the quay. An old man was, indeed, there, putting out the green light which had frightened the cubs as they crossed, but he was as deaf as his ladder, and before he approached the edge to see how high the tide had risen, they had made their greatest effort and gained the shelter of the masonry.

That day they hardly slept a wink. They were within earshot of the busiest spot in the port, and every one of the varied sounds that reached them was a cause for fresh anxiety. To the ceaseless pacing to and fro of hobbler and pilot there was soon added the shout of the fish hawker, the bell of the town-crier, and other sounds of trade, varied towards noon by the squeakings of Punch and Judy, the yelping of Toby, and the roars of laughter that punctuated their performance – a strange hullabaloo indeed for the shy wildlings that had been reared in the quiet of the desolate moorland, where only the calls of bird and beast reached them; and many a time through the trying hours they longed to be back in the morass, under the cairn, or in the cave now so far back on the trail. Welcome at last to their eyes were the dying rays that fired the windows of the cottages across the harbour; doubly welcome the departure of the last fisherman from the quay-head. His footsteps had scarcely died away when the otters slid down the face of the wall into the water and, threading the moorings of the boats above them, rose to the surface in the fairway. Three dark spots that to the man leaning over the side of the brigantine might well have seemed three corks, showed where the otters swam noiselessly towards the harbour-mouth.

After they had passed the last buoy and, indeed, covered most of the mile that separated them from the lighthouse, they learnt that they were not the only creatures abroad that fine summer night. Barely a furlong could have separated them from the castles that once guarded the narrow entrance when they caught sight of some monsters whose noisy breathing, growing louder and louder as they drew near, might well have proved most terrifying to the easily scared cubs, had not their mother's indifference convinced them they had nothing to fear; and presently mother and cubs were among the shoal of porpoises, the great backs of which gleamed as they showed above the waves. The mother knew the errand of these corsairs, and understood that they were raiding the salmon that the flooded river had attracted from the offing. Awakened memories of great chases in the pools and of feasts on the banks flashed across her brain as she swam, and before she set foot on the point opposite the lighthouse she resolved to complete the round with as little delay as possible and regain the upper reaches of the river, where she could teach the cubs how to weary out the fresh-run fish and bring them to the bank.

But the lesson she had come to give the cubs in the sea itself was not a whit less important, she thought, as she watched their wonderment on beholding the vast liquid plain that stretched out to no shore their piercing gaze could discern. Streamlet, pool, river, creek, estuary – all in turn had been cause for astonishment, but on the ocean they looked with awe. And it was theirs to fish in. In the recognition of this spacious hunting-ground the timid creatures quite forgot the terrors of the quay, which had but momentarily passed from their minds in the presence of the porpoises, and the next minute they were following in the wake of their mother as she swam towards the Gull Rock in the midst of the cliff-skirted bay. Bravely the cubs faced the waves, and bravely they battled with the surf through which they landed; then they looked to their mother to direct them how to fish in the deep water by which they were surrounded.

They had not long to wait. After a glance at the birds on the ledges above her head, she dived; both cubs instantly dived, too, and putting forth all the strength of their hind-legs, they succeeded in keeping her in sight along the spiral course by which she made her way down and down to the bottom, full six fathoms below. To their surprise, they found the bed of the sea alive with tiny shell-fish, which they spurned here and there as they quested. On their left rose a wall of rock, in turning the point of which they came face to face with a turbot, that the otter seized and bore writhing to the surface. The cubs, who rose with her, kept gripping the fish as they swam, and by the time they reached the landing-place it had ceased to struggle. Then all three settled down to the feast. Nothing but the tail and backbone remained when they again took to the water. This time they made the circuit of the rock, and the male cub, rising from beneath, seized a pollack, carried it in triumph to a reef just a-wash with the tide, and there consumed it. Before he had quite finished, the other cub, and later, the otter, were busy devouring wrasse they had taken. When they had eaten their fill, the young otters amused themselves in capturing fish which they no longer needed but left uneaten; and it was over these abandoned spoils that the gulls clamoured at dawn, whilst the otters lay in a cave they had entered by a submerged mouth at the foot of the cliffs. Curled up in pits on the sand above the line of flotsam, with the roar of the sea to lull them, the cubs soon dropped asleep; but the mother, her thoughts on the big silvery salmon, lay awake making her plans, till at length she, too, yielded to her fatigue and slept like the cubs.

Night had fallen when the otters stole through the outlet, left half uncovered by the ebb, and swam with rapid strokes for the head of the bay. They were off to a new fishing-ground. They landed where a stream crosses the beach and, striking into the valley down which it flows, followed its course without a halt, until they reached the junction of the two rivulets that form it. There, however, the otter stood irresolute. Each water led towards a delectable destination – the one to the salmon pools, the other to her native marsh, with its abundant food-supply and secure hovers among the reed-beds – and which to make for she could not decide, until it struck her that the cubs might never find the outlying water without her. Then she set aside her hesitation, and held along the western branch at a pace quicker than before, as if to recover the time lost in making up her mind.

Leaving the valley about a mile above the confluence, she cut straight across the middle of the hilly field to the upper corner, where a flock of lambs stood awestruck to watch the strange intruders climb the bank into the next pasture, from which the otters could hear the startled creatures stamping with excitement, until first the otter, then the cubs one after the other, got over the wall and dropped into a neglected road. This led to a stately gateway with big iron gates, and beneath them the animals crept to the moss-grown drive, flecked by the moonlight which filtered through the arching crowns of the oaks. They passed a mole-heap or two and numerous little pits scratched by rabbits, but the way was innocent of rut or hoof-mark or any evidence of man's proximity. Yet they had not long been following its windings before they all at once found themselves face to face with a scene that filled them with consternation. At a spot where the road makes a sharp bend about an angle of the cliff lay a heap of ruddy embers, and near them a dog. The animal was not asleep, but stretched to his full length and, as his restless ears showed, alert to the slightest sound. His every movement was visible against the dying fire, the glow of which fell on the curtained window of a caravan and dimly revealed the gnarled branches above it. The otters, thoroughly alive to the danger of attack, stood ready to defend themselves; but, seeing that the enemy gave no sign, they sidled towards the overgrown riding-path just beyond the firelight, and gained it without attracting the dog's attention. The moment, however, the herbage rustled with their movements his head was raised and pointed towards the very spot where they stood concealed. Still as death, they regarded the lurcher through the fronds, nor did they advance a single step till the drooping of the pricked ears and the resettling of the long head on the fore-legs showed that suspicion was lulled. Then, with a stealth that cheated the prating ferns, they left their shelter, stole noiselessly as shadows past the gipsy's bivouac and the side road by which the human nomads had come, and escaped into the safe darkness beyond, where, the murmur of the sea far below reached their ears.

After passing the haunted house to which the long avenue led, they came to a cairn with a roofless lookout, so placed as to survey the wild coast-line. Here the wanderers again struck inland until they came to a high wall that threatened to bar their advance. But the otter knew the way and, threading the nettles bordering the stubble, reached the drain that gives easy access to the park. As if glad to be clear of the prickly harvest-field, the little band made down the slope at a gallop, passing between groups of trees that cast deep shadows on the turf. In the herbage of the hollow only their backs showed, but every hair was exposed when they breasted the opposite slope, over whose crest the land dips abruptly to a fishpond. At a headlong pace they dashed between the stems of the pines to the edge of the water, into which they glided as noiselessly as voles. So swift were their movements that almost before their presence was known each otter had seized a white trout and risen to the surface. One came up near the boathouse, another in the shadow of an hydrangea, the third near the only bit of moonlit bank by the overflow; and all three swam towards the island, where they lay under the plumes of the pampas-grass and devoured their take. They ate three or four fish apiece before their hunger was satisfied, and then began chasing one another over the rocks, from which the sea stretched like a plain of beaten silver. Soon they returned along the overflow to the pond, where they gambolled as fearlessly as they had done in the creek and other lone spots in their wanderings.

To the surprise of the cubs, the taint of man on the path caused their mother no disquietude; not once did she stop her play to listen or peer into the bosky gloom about her. Strange disregard of danger in a creature both suspicious and apprehensive, yet not difficult of explanation. For all the demesne within the park wall had long been a sanctuary for bird and beast. Not a gun had been fired there nor a trap set time out of mind; and so confiding had even otters become that they used the drain on the island to litter in, and would lay up in the holt by the moat under the very windows of the mansion.

Behind one of these a light had just before been burning, where the young squire sat recording the day's sport with his hounds along the stream in which the otter had taught the cubs to fish. But as he wrote he heard the otter whistle. On the instant he dropped his pen, turned down the lamp and seizing a field-glass, took his seat by the open window. Keen otter hunter as he was, he was no less keen a naturalist. Deer, foxes, badgers, seals, all interested him, though not to the same degree as the otter. The fascination this creature had for him was wonderful. To him it was the homeless hunter, the Bedouin of the wild, the subtlest and most enduring of quarry, the gamest of the game. Therefore he sat with glass to eye watching the lighted space between two clumps of rhododendrons where he expected the otters would show. His hands shook and his heart beat faster than its wont; for the life of him he could not suppress the excitement he felt. Presently a shadow, a moving shadow, followed by another and yet another, darkened the sward – these were the otters; and without a wink he watched them cross the turf to the ferny border of the moat, where, though he could see them no longer, he could follow their movements by the twitching of the fronds till, a few seconds later, they entered the water and pursued their graceful gambols full in his view. Once the otter, attracted by scent or sound, or both, half rose out of the moat and looked over the low bank; but the moment she saw that the intruders were only a badger and two cubs she fell again to her romps. Later she looked up and scrutinized the strange object at the window. The squire remained as motionless as the gargoyles; her suspicion was allayed, and once more she resumed her frolics. Anon the trio stole away and, passing through the drain beneath the park wall by which the badgers had found an entrance, gained the valley where the weary hounds lay asleep in their kennels. But without a thought of hound or anything else save the marsh to which she was hurrying, the otter made across the barren holdings beyond and, before the squire had given up hope of their reappearance and resumed his pen, she had dropped from the boundary wall of Cold Comfort Farm and set foot on the waste that stretches to the very tip of the promontory.

The wanderers kept near the cliffs, going straight from angle to angle of the indentations that mark the jagged coast-line. Here and there they moved along the edge, so close one behind the other as to look like one creature, presenting even, at times, a snake-like appearance, especially when twisting in and out of the colony of ant-heaps that dotted the long slope within a mile of their destination. Near the top they disturbed a wheatear from amongst some cushions of withered sea-pinks; but not another creature did they see until abreast of the seal rock, where a cormorant stood watching for the dawn. Then, striking the marsh at the end of a finger-like creek, they followed the bank above it till the mere with its reed-beds lay before them. Not a breath ruffled the surface: the array of stems stood motionless as forest-trees: all was strangely still, save that the sea was heaving ominously. After a keen scrutiny of the cottage opposite them and a single glance at the sand-bar to the left, the otter trotted down the bank and, entering the water, swam towards the farther shore. But when near the wall of reeds she half-wheeled, and coasted along the curves of the little bays, skirting the lily-beds where she had disported when a cub.

Till now the finny tenants of the mere had given no sign of their presence; but as the otters drew near the inflow a dace jumped out of the water, and the jaws of a pike showed above the surface within a few inches of it. The sight stirred the hunting instincts of the male cub, and so great was his rage at his mother's indifference that, when she crossed the current on her way to the creek, he turned back, determined to hover by himself. He landed on a point between two bays and trampled a couch at the foot of the reeds. An old otter could not have chosen a kennel seemingly safer, yet scarcely had he curled up when a most alarming noise struck his ears. It was the creak of oars against the thole-pins, and it grew louder and louder till he jumped to his feet to see what was coming. Almost immediately the bow of a boat appeared round a clump of bulrushes, and at the oars bent the old marshman in his reed-plaited hat and guernsey frock, all lit up by the red sun, now just above the bar. The rower shipped the oars, turned round on his seat, and dropped the killick quietly overboard; but the boat still moved forward till the painter stopped the way on it, less than a score of yards from the otter, who looked on at the baiting and setting of the lines, and even the lighting of a pipe before the old man settled down to watch the floats.

Motionless though the fisherman sat, the otter remained on the alert and, whenever the old man rose to land a fish, was on the point of diving and making his escape from so dangerous a neighbour. Thus hour after hour passed, and the morning wore away with no change in the situation, save that a little before noon black clouds rose above the horizon and drifted into the blue spaces of the sky. Intent on his fishing, the marshman took little notice of the sudden change of weather, until a gust of wind shook the reed-bed and big drops of rain began to fall. Then, casting a few uneasy glances to windward, he pulled in his lines, raised the killick, pressed his hat on his head, and rowed away.

THE FAMILY
BROKEN UP

ᐱᔆ

S ITTING THERE, THE CUB WATCHED the lurid after-glow fade, dusk creep over the rough water, and the sky darken till a star appeared in a break between the scudding wrack. Then he rose and listened. The waves broke against the point, the reeds hissed, the breakers thundered on the bar, but no call from his mother reached his eager ears. He was beginning to fear she had deserted him when from across the mere came the shrill summons. Immediately he dived and, rising almost at once, headed at excited pace for the creek, where soon, to his delight, he viewed his mother and sister swimming to meet him. The wild gambols that followed in the midst of the mere did not last long, for there was hunting to be done.

The quarry the otter had set her mind on were the pike frequenting the reedy bays, towards the largest of which the hunters swam. Near a bed of lilies they dived, and had not made half the circuit of the wall of stems before they espied a pike. He had already seen them, and in an instant the protruding muzzle was withdrawn as the fish backed into his ambush. It afforded him no refuge from the pursuers, who drove him from one to another of its recesses, and pressed him so closely that, as he saw, to remain meant capture. Out he flashed and, had he made right away and gained the heart of the mere, he would have escaped. But he sought the shelter of another lily-bed almost within sight of the first, and there the otters followed in unrelenting chase. Presently he was gripped by the male cub, but, freeing himself, forsook the weeds for the water outside, where, with distended jaws and fins erect, he darted now here, now there, to avoid his harassing pursuers. All was in vain. He had missed his earlier opportunities, and to escape in his exhausted condition was impossible. Conscious of this and determined not to die unavenged, he summoned his remaining strength, dashed at the otter, seized her by the throat, and held on despite her struggles. This however left him at the mercy of the cubs. Instantly they fastened on his shoulders and, using their powerful rudders, tried to raise him to the surface. Beating his tail, the fish for awhile succeeded in resisting their efforts; but in the end he tired, and presently the writhing mass came to the top of the lake and, rolling over and over, showed now on the crest, now in the trough of the waves. There the otter wrenched herself free and, half-throttled though she was, at once joined in the attack. The three soon overpowered their prey and landed with it at an opening in the reeds. Whilst they were dragging it from the water's edge a tremor passed through the fish. Immediately the hungry hunters relaxed their hold, fell to and sliced and sliced and champed and champed till wellnigh half the fish was eaten and the great backbone showed. The feast over, they licked their chops, brushed their whiskers against the stems and, taking to the water, played hide-and-seek amongst the lilies.

The exultation they felt over their capture showed in their excited gambols and in their wild rush through the reed-bed on their way to the bar. They crossed this at a gallop to the edge of the tide, plunged into the breakers and, reaching the quieter water beyond the surf, headed straight for the great pile of rocks over which the spray was dashing in clouds. On landing, they threaded the sobbing passages between the boulders and gained the caves that honeycomb the cliff behind. There they came on the remains of old feasts – fish bones, crab and lobster shells – and on old nests made of reeds. One cave there was where the muffled boom of the waves was broken by the tinkle of falling water, and where the skeletons of otters whitened the floor on the edge of the runlet that had worn a channel in the rock. Quickly leaving it, the animals made their way back along the low, tortuous passage by which they had entered and, passing through the outer caves, regained the clitter. There they chased one another until they tired. Then they took to the sea, reached the line of the breakers, and landed through the welter as easily as, later, they landed on the bank of the mere by the inflow. The otter was then leading her cubs to the withy-bed and to the boggy ground between it and the old decoy, where she trod the water-mint as she went.

So the hours of darkness were spent, and when the grey light told of coming day otter and cubs slipped into the stream and drifted towards the mere. On reaching the choppy water they fell to swimming, turned up the sheltered creek, skirted the island where two of them had kennelled the day before, and landed near a bramble brake, in which they curled up side by side. The cubs soon slept, but the excitement of the journey to the salmon river kept the otter awake longing for dusk, so eager was she to cross the moors and reach the pools. She dropped asleep at last, but awoke long before setting-out time and, whilst awaiting nightfall, watched the angry sun go down and the clouds scud by close overhead.

Before it was quite dark she aroused the cubs, and made up the hilly ground towards the heart of the moor. It was a wild night, but the fury of the gale seemed to quicken the energies of the wanderers, for they breasted the foothills at a pace beyond their wont and soon gained the high plateau with its chain of pools, known to men as the Black Liddens. These they swam as they came to them, passed to the heathery waste with its old Stone Circle, and reached the marshy valley and the lazy stream which supplies the mere. The wind had little force there – the thorns, shaggy with lichen, stood motionless, even the bulrushes scarcely stirred; but over a stagnant backwater a will-o'-the-wisp kept dancing like a lantern swung by invisible hands. Splash! splash! the otters crossed the shallow pool near the stream; and again, splash! splash! they rushed through the shoal water beyond it before turning up the brae that led to the wind-swept moor. On, on the untiring creatures sped, more like agents of darkness executing some urgent commission than beasts of prey speeding to a new fishing-ground. Mile after mile of the desolate upland they traversed: at one spot skirting a cairn whence came that weirdest of all wild cries, the shrill chattering of badgers; at another, passing the only road over the moor, where they left their footprints between the fresh wheel-marks of the doctor's trap. A sleeping hamlet rose almost in their path, and so close did they approach that they heard the creaking of the signboard of the Druid's Arms, about which the cottages cluster. Then over wall after wall they clambered as they came to the crofters' holdings, reached the lodge of the keeper who had been the otter's terror when her cubs were helpless, gained the edge of the moorland above the old nursery, made their way down the very gully along which the hounds had followed the fox and, leaping the stream close to the hover, came out on the salmon pool beyond the poplar.

Eager to see whether the pool held a fish, the otter slipped into the water and swam to the favourite lie near the foot of the fall. A salmon was there, and towards it she advanced so swiftly that it seemed she must fasten before it could become aware of her presence. But the fish had been harried by otters on its way up from the estuary, and was prepared for her coming. In a flash he was off downstream, leaving the otter far in his wake. At the tail of the pool he swung round, raising a big wave that greatly excited the cubs where they watched on the edge of the bank. After a short interval the wave came again, and again, and again. Later the salmon leapt clear of the white water near the fall. And so the chase continued, until the otter, seeing how vain were her unaided efforts, summoned the cubs to her assistance. In an instant they slipped into the pool and joined in the pursuit.

Now wherever the salmon turns an otter meets him. Conscious of the danger he is in, he rushes at the shallows in a daring attempt to reach the waters below. His three enemies hurry after him, breaking the surface in their desperate haste, and while he is still floundering the otter closes and strives to grip him beneath the gills. No defence has he but his slippery scales and the lashing tail that sweeps his foes aside. But these avail, and before the teeth fasten in him he struggles through to the deep water beyond, where he easily outdistances his pursuers. Pool after pool he passes at his utmost speed, making for a refuge that lies near the foot of the rapids. He had rested in it on his way up the river, and now swings into it and stays there gasping, in dread of discovery. The otters soon show on the top of the rushing waters, which they search as they descend, ducking their heads, and yet avoiding the rocks against which the current threatens to dash them. In a few seconds they are close to the spot where the fish lies exhausted, and surely one or other will get a glimpse of him. But no, the sheltering rock befriends him, or the foaming waters amidst which he lies. The hunters pass on; but he is not safe yet. If they draw the rapids against the stream they can hardly miss him. But will they? Apparently not – at least, not for the moment. They are going on, despite the near approach of day. How carefully they examine the hollow banks and recesses of the boulders, disdaining even the grilse they disturb, in their expectation of yet getting the salmon! Beneath the gloomy pines that form a vista towards the brightening east they swim, eager as ever.

But, clear of the trees, they all at once cease their quest and listen. Some suspicious sound downstream has alarmed them. They are all ears when, above the voice of the river and the wild rustling of the tree-tops, the penetrating note again makes itself heard. It is the toot of the horn. The twice-hunted otter dreads that sound above all sounds save the cry of the hounds, and before it has died away she and the cubs are in full retreat to the holt in the salmon pool. Only at long intervals do they rise to vent before reaching the rapids, where they leave the water and gallop up the bank, as if fear itself were at their heels. At the top they re-enter the river, and so gain the shelter of the alder-roots near the fall.

The cubs, feeling safe in the holt, make their toilet as usual: but the otter listens, and before long catches the dreaded cry. Then the cubs hear it too: they begin to share their mother's alarm and, when the swelling clamour tells of the close approach of their enemies, seek the inmost recess of their refuge. Soon the hounds enter the pool and cluster like maddened things about the holt. 'A good solid mark,' shouts the doctor to the squire. 'He's there right enough.' The foremost hounds can see the otter where she stands hissing through her white teeth, but they cannot reach her. So the hounds are called off that a terrier may get at the quarry, and after a terrible fight he compels the otter to take to the water. Shouts of 'Heu gaz' from the field greet the appearance of the bubbles that betray her flight, and the next moment the twelve couple of hounds are in pursuit towards the stickle, where a dozen men or more stand foot to foot to prevent her from going down-water. Round and round the big pool swims the otter, rising now under the bank, now amongst the hounds, narrowly escaping their jaws. Time after time she returns to the cubs, but only to be ejected by one or other terriers. At last, after being badly shaken by the hounds, she lands, gallops round the line of men with the white terrier at her rudder, and gains the water beyond. At amazing speed she follows the winding reaches to the rapids, and even succeeds in gaining Longen Pool, famous in the annals of the Hunt. However, the hounds again press her sorely, and after a while she takes to the tangled coppice on the hillside, traverses it, reaches an ancient hedgerow batted with bramble and thorn, and there lies listening, trusting to have escaped pursuit. But she has left a burning scent, and soon the cry of the pursuers warns her that her hopes are vain. Nevertheless, as she is very weary, and as the pool to which the hedge runs down offers no harbourage, she remains where she is. But though the hounds soon wind her, the denseness of the thicket hinders them from getting at her until the terriers force her to the river. In the shallow water every eye can mark her where she swims and note her shortening dives. The end is near. Presently Dosmary seizes her as she rises, and the pack worries her life out.

That night, when the storm had passed, the miller heard the cries of the two otters in the tangled coppice beyond the orchard, and as he knocked the ashes from his pipe before going indoors, said: 'They're missin' her, I'm thinkin'.' He was right. It was the voice of the cubs calling for their mother.

They were there again the next night, and the next; after that they gave up the vain search and withdrew to the moorland.

It was well for the young creatures, thus thrown on their own resources, that they were able to fend for themselves. Indeed, as has been seen, the male cub had already shown signs of revolt against his mother's authority, and of a desire for independence.

He was free now, free to roam as he liked, to keep to the trail or leave it as he pleased, to fish when and where he chose; for his sister had no influence over him. Yet, for all his selfish, headstrong ways, he proved a safe leader, his movements being inspired by the wariness of the outlawed creature. He was a stickler for good hours, rising late and couching early. He curbed his passion for wandering, and showed rare judgement in the choice of hovers, selecting always with an eye to strength and invariably shunning such as were not near deep water where refuge might be sought in emergency. On sallying out he generally fished upstream for a mile or two, gambolled till the night was nearly gone, and then floated back with the current, shooting the rapids and lesser falls on the way. Yet fear haunted both him and his sister, for they carefully scrutinized every bush, rock, and bole that might harbour an enemy, and their fears grew to terror once when they happened on the remains of one of their kind recently killed by the hounds. On the discovery they were at once all consternation, as their puffing and blowing showed, and forthwith forsook the tributary for the river, kennelling at the end of their hurried retreat in a hover below the mill. They lay in this holt on the following day, but the next found them ensconced under the bank of the weir pool at Tide End. There they were waked towards noon by the tide, which rose and rose till it invaded their quarters, and compelled them to seek refuge in the opposite bank, where a young dog-otter was already lying up. Their coming startled him not a little, but the moment he saw the new arrivals were otters like himself he settled down again, and soon all three were sound asleep. At dusk they journeyed on together and, after fishing and sporting in the salmon pool below the morass, sought the roots of the alder. They lay there again on the morrow, a morrow momentous in one of its happenings – the separation of the cubs. For when, at setting-out time, the male cub began moving up-water, his sister, till that moment the most faithful of followers, turned her back on him and, with the strange otter at her heels, struck into the wood. She had renounced the brother for the lover. Is it possible, animal though she is, that she can abandon the companion of her life hitherto, without some sign of regret? May not the slowness of her steps indicate reluctance to sever the ties that have so long bound them? Surely it is so, for just as she is about to enter the under-growth, she stops and turns her head to find her brother watching her. The next minute, however, she has passed out of his sight and out of his life, as, with her mate, she follows the trail that leads by the woodman's cottage and the cairn to the distant mussel creek whither she is bound.

CHAPTER SEVEN

THE OTTER
AT THE TARN

ح۶

S O THE OTTER HELD ON HIS WAY alone, and before dawn broke sought shelter in the wooded ravine next the edge of the moor.

The rocky recess was one of the favourite holts of his kind, partly on account of the dry lying it afforded, but more because of its congenial surroundings. The seclusion, the gloom, the roar of the fall, and the tumult of the pool all contributed to please the shy wildling; and he became so fond of the ledge by the foaming waters that, like a badger to its earth, the young nomad returned to it again and again, till at length the instinct to roam began to cry out against his unnatural conduct and urged him to seek new quarters. 'Wander, wander,' repeated the voice that grew more insistent as the days stole by. 'Tarry, my child, tarry,' replied the spirit of the glen; and for a while – a little while – he resolved to stay. Yet before his short sojourn came to an end the pool was sought by a hunted stag and turned into a pandemonium.

Not by mere chance, after rounding the base of Lone Tarn, was the beast's antlered head set for the ravine. It was there he had first seen the light. The early weeks of his life had been spent in the ferny clearing where the otter's trail ran, and his mother used to lead him, a dappled calf, down the steep bank to drink at the shallows of the otter's pool. Four years had passed since then; but the memory of the sombre, sequestered glen and of the pool at the foot of the high fall was still clear in his mind, and to them he turned his wearied steps in the hour of his distress. After crossing the rugged purlieus of the woodland, he threaded his way between the stems of the birches and, entering the ravine at its lower end, made his way up and up along the shaded waters until he came opposite the holt, where a submerged rock permitted foothold. His wild rush through the shallows had filled the startled sleeper with alarm; but the otter did not understand the cause of the strange creature's distress until the cry of the pursuers caught his ears – a cry that swelled louder and louder until every hound had splashed into the pool and swam there, baying their quarry with deafening clamour. More than once whilst the din was at its height the otter was on the point of slipping into the water and stealing away; but it was well he refrained, for presently the stag broke its bay and made off down the river, drawing the pack after it.

Then, though calm returned to the pool from which it had been so ruthlessly banished, it brought no peace to the otter. A peel leaped where the stag had stood, trout rose where the hounds had clustered, pigeons 'roohooed' overhead, and a squirrel came down and drank at the water, yet the otter was still perturbed. His faith in the holt was gone, and he longed for dusk that he might leave it and get away from the taint of hound that drowned the scent of moss and fern and poisoned the sweet, fresh breath of the river. He did not await the fall of night, for a faint glow yet lighted the spaces between the boles when he left, and as he came out upon the moor, the sky was still red with the embers of sunset. Far ahead loomed the familiar outline of the solitary hill, as yet unvisited; and now at last he determined to follow the stream that veined it to the summit, and there find the refuge that the specious ravine denied.

At a good pace he moved over the heather and bog till, a furlong or so beyond some stacks of turf, he came to a sudden standstill. It seemed as if he had caught come suspicious sound along the back trail, for his head was suddenly turned that way; but, discerning nothing, he resumed his brisk trot along the bank that at this point rose high above the rushing river. Soon he came to the tributary down which his mother had led him and, swimming Moor Pool, as the meeting of the waters is called, he crossed to the opposite bank and kept it till he reached the troubled 'Kieve' at the base of the hill. As though haunted by the memory of the hounds, he again looked back over the moor, now black under the stars; but in the end, after peering long and satisfying himself that no enemy followed his trail, he slipped into the foaming basin in search of the trout it contained, and on two of these fish made a hurried supper before beginning the climb of the great cone that towered grim and forlorn above him. He kept close to the wild, headlong stream, and made the ascent by scrambling up the rocks that abutted on fall and cascade. Far, far up, his nostrils caught the scent of a body of water, and in his eagerness to reach it he redoubled his pace and soon gained the crest. There he found himself face to face with a tarn – a tarn of aspect as forbidding as the strangely contrasted shores that encompass it, for the sheet of water lies sullen and monotonous between precipitous rocks and a beach of grey shingle. No islet rears its head above the surface; no line of flotsam marks the shelving strand. The wanderer had come out on the shingly beach, and after sniffing the water he trotted leisurely along its edge, and presently descried a small bed of reeds, till then hidden by a rocky headland. Gladdened by the discovery, he mended his pace, yet kept surveying the tarn, doubtless on the lookout for signs of prey. A wave in the shallows, a splash, or even a dimple, any break of the water, would have betrayed the presence of some finny inhabitant, of which, however, his nose had given him no hint; but the surface had no message for him. Neither was there a single wild-fowl; there was no animal of any sort. At the far end, however, and almost in his path as he made the circuit of the pool, lay the skeleton of a giant pike. Though the vertebrae had dropped into crannies between the stones, the bleached skull, its open jaws bristling with teeth, was the most conspicuous object on that desolate shore. Yet dry bones apparently had no more interest for him than the newly risen moon, for he passed on and clambered over the rocks towards the reeds, where he was soon at work preparing a couch in which to pass the coming day. The unusual noise awoke a buzzard in his eyrie above, and kept him awake until the otter ceased trampling the stems and entered the water; then he lowered his head on his wing and dropped asleep again.

The otter, meanwhile, swam towards the horn of the bay, his long back flush with the surface, scarce rippled by his advance. When clear of the point, he dived and began exploring the recesses and ledges. There was not a harbourage along the cliff's base that he did not investigate, but he did not sight a single fish. Reaching the glassy surface by the overflow, he spreadeagled himself and drifted more and more quickly towards the lip of the fall, till it seemed that nothing could save him from going over; but within a foot or two of the brink he suddenly wheeled, and extricated himself by rapid strokes that took him within a score yards of the beach. Then he dived again and quested along the stretch between the shallows and the deep. This likely hunting-ground also proved as void of fish as the water under the cliff; so at the farther end he landed, shook his coat, and rolled on the shingle, thus catching the skull of the pike, which he sent flying over the stones. The rattle it made caused him to run after it, and the grim toy served to amuse him, for he played with it much as a kitten plays with a ball.

Not so had its owner been bandied about by his forebears. More than one otter, appalled by his great bulk and terrible jaws, had shrunk from tackling him: even the father of the cub was glad, after a tussle that convulsed the little bay, to reach the rocks and escape with his life. But famine had effected what no enemy could effect – a famine caused by the ravages of otter, of heron, of cormorant, of the pike themselves, reducing the fish one by one till only the monster of the reedy bay remained. Whilst strength lasted he made a daily circuit of his wasted realm for prey to sat-isfy his maddening hunger. As his weakness increased, his beat dwindled, until one day, after but a short cruise, it was all he could do to regain his station among the reeds. There he lingered till death claimed him. His gaunt carcass, still beautiful with its marblings of olive and gold, rose to the surface, and the west wind wafted it to the strand, where the terror of one generation became the sport of the next.

The otter, however, soon tired of toying with the skull and, leaving it where he found it, he made along the rocks towards the spot where the precipice rises almost sheer from the tarn, and began to scour the face of the cliff. He seemed as surefooted as a marten, and never once slipped or stumbled as he dropped from shelf to shelf whose scanty width in places all but denied foothold.

Three times he made the descent, leaping from ledge to ledge like
the overflow rushing down the hillside; but, unlike the stream, he
leaped in silence, save for the muffled thud of his spongy feet as
they struck the rock on landing. The last time he dived, rose at the
end of a long swim by the boulder flanking the outlet, climbed to
the top, and lay down at full length. The water ran from his
unshaken coat, leaving it smooth and refulgent in the moonlight,
as he reposed there gazing at the windings of the river on the plain
below. Soon however the restless creature rose and plunged again
into the tarn, where he gambolled, partly on the surface, but
chiefly beneath amongst the currents that well up from the
unfathomed depths. And so the hours sped till, when the moon
had set and the stars wellnigh paled, he gave over disporting himself and swam towards his lair. On the way thither, forgetting that
he was alone, he uttered the dawn cry, and the next moment
rounded the point and gained the reeds. In the grey light, the buzzard winging his way to the moorland saw him curled up there,
holding one of his pads in his mouth – asleep, as he knew by the
slow, regular rise and fall of his flank.

But what creature is that astir near the outlet? It must be some
other wildling come to share the primal solitude of the hilltop. Yet
its movements are not those of a four-footed beast. Surely, surely
it is a – is it possible? Yes, it is a man! He is clear of the rocks now,
and is picking his way across the current. Now he has landed, and
look, look how he hurries up the strand, and how suddenly he
drops to the ground on the crest! Strange conduct in this lone
place and at such an hour! He must be under the ban of his fellows, a fugitive, maybe, from hue and cry, and fearful of discovery.

Nothing of the kind. That man is Grylls the harbourer, from the
deer forest; but otter, not stag, has drawn him here this morning,

84

and eagerness to examine the ground below is the reason of his haste. Already, glass to eye, he follows the course of the tributary on his left, hopeful every second of seeing an otter making its way to the clitter near the stream. How carefully he scans the banks, and what a time he dwells on the pile of hoary rocks yet spectral in the uncertain light! 'No luck, no luck,' he mutters, as he turns the glass to the tributary zigzagging across the western moor. Yet he is all expectation, and great will be his joy if only he can get a glimpse of the long, dark creature hieing to some holt. Away up to the boggy gathering ground he traces the narrowing water, surveys in vain the pools amidst that curlew-haunted waste, then with quick movement, redirects the glass to the clitter, already much less dim and mysterious. Little wonder that that particular refuge attracts him so strongly, that he scrutinizes the approaches so carefully. It was there that he once marked an otter enter; and the memory of the sport it gave has drawn him year after year to the hilltop in the hope of harbouring another. Again and again he surveys first one stream, then the other, but with no better result; then he hurriedly examines the river from the foot of the hill to Moor Pool, where the hounds will presently meet. 'Nothin' movin', nothin' at all, and day close handy. You may as well shut up the glass.' Soon the fleecy clouds crowding the vault are tinged with rose, pool and stream catch the foreglow, the reflection in the tarn is like an almond grove in bloom, and the sun shows below the crimson streaks that had heralded it. At the sight Grylls returns the glass to his pocket and, feeling chilled, jumps to his feet and walks briskly up and down on the rim of the great basin to warm himself.

Had he seen an otter he would by this be crossing the moor to meet the squire and tell, instead of pacing to and fro waiting for the hounds and glancing down now and again towards the spot where he expects to see them. It is full day by this, and river and tributary stream stretch across the purple moorland like golden threads. 'Grand mornin'. Ah! if we can only find!' he sighed, as the uncertainty of the sport flashed across his mind. 'If! But there, man, 'tes no use iffin'. Wait and hope for the best.' All at once the harbourer stopped and, screwing up his eyes, looked steadily towards the solitary clump of pines to which from time to time he had directed his gaze. 'Here they come, and a good few with 'em. Ah! ah! and there's one, two, three, four comin' up-river, and Matthey – it can't be anybody else – crossing the foord. There'll be a brave little meet to end the season.' Then he lay down again on the heather, raised the glass to his eye, and turned it on the party with the hounds. 'The squire and the passun, of coorse. Wonder if church moosic or hound cry do stir un most.' "Everything in its season, Grylls," that would be his answer, and said kindly. He is a good sort, is the passun, and dearly loves a kill. And theere's Doctor Jim, in his white hat. Lor'! he ain't missed the Moor Pool meet for seven-and-thirty years. Iss, seven-and-thirty year. Grylls, and it's seven-and-thirty times you've sat where you're sittin' now to the hour, and wellnigh to the day, and' – counting the notches on his stick – 'it's nine otters you've seen killed on the moor. Who can they be with the Doctor? Strainyers, I reckon, stayin' at the big house most like. Ah! theere's Black Geordie, and the keeper, and the landlord, and Tom "Burn the Reed" walkin' with the bailiff hisself as large as life and as brazen as Sally Strout at the christenin'. Well, he's got a face, and no mistake! Wonder how many salmin he's took out this turn.'

Thus he lay and made his comments whilst the party approached Moor Pool, but no sooner did they reach the bank than his demeanour changed and he sprang to his feet as though an adder had stung him. And no wonder, for the hounds at once struck the line of the otter, and made down-river at full cry. 'Well now, Grylls,' said he, 'is it go or stay? Why, stay, of coorse; sure as you're alive they'll be back again.' So he stood watching and watching and watching till hounds and men became blurred by distance, and at last disappeared into the wood. 'You're out of it, git chucklehead!' said he, as he lowered the glass. 'Why didn't 'ee go down to the meet as you always do? You're getting' lazy. You're out of it, out of it, and come fifteen mile for nothin'! Pick up the pony and shog home along; there's nothin' else for 'ee to do.' In his rage he kicked the loose rock at his feet, and sent it bounding down the face of the hill. Nevertheless, it was not many seconds before he was again scrutinizing the spot where the river falls to the ravine, and before long he exclaimed, 'Halloo! what's that? Ah, theere 'tes again and again; the glint of the horn, I'll be bound.' He was all excitement now, and watching as he had never watched before in his life. 'What's that – eh, eh? It's they, it's they! See, thee're crossin' the bend of Zingey Pool.' Though the hounds were scarcely discernible he was right: they were returning and becoming more and more distinct every minute. 'Hoorah,' he shouted in his exultation; 'the otter must have come up-water laast night; wheere's he lyin', wonder.' His eyes, almost starting from his head, followed the pack as it drew nearer and nearer to Moor Pool. They reached it; then he was all anxiety to see whether they would take up the tributary or keep to the river. Like a man toeing the line for a foot-race he stood ready to start, and if they had gone up the stream he would have descended the hill at breakneck speed; but they did not: they came on. 'Niver such a bit of luck in all my born days,' said he, his weather-beaten face beaming with delight. Presently, as the deep bay, like the bay of blood-hounds, reached his ears:

'What moosic! how wild and savage and grand it is! eh, and what a sight for one pair of eyes! The squire'd give gold to be in my shoes.' Not for a single instant did the harbourer divert his gaze from the pack. 'Pretty, pretty,' he kept saying as the hounds, time after time, recovered the line momentarily lost. 'They're travellin' fast. It's time to be going down. I'll lay a groat the otter's in the Kieve.' With a bound he was off and, following the overflow, had just reached the big boulder from which the buzzard sometimes watched the moor, when, to his surprise, he saw Dosmary and Tuneful just beginning the ascent of the hill.

'Niver lyin' up round the tarn! 'Tes ten year agone since they found theere. However, here they come, here the beauties come.'

There was a strange tenderness in his voice, but the light that leapt to his eyes told still more plainly how he was stirred. He watched them for a few moments, so that the whole pack was in sight before he began retracing his steps, and quickly as his sinewy legs carried him up the steep, the hounds had passed him when he gained the crest. Quivering with excitement, he stood again for a moment with his eyes on them as they streamed along the strand; then he tore along in their wake.

He might have covered twoscore yards, during which the pack had swept round the end of the tarn to the rocks, when a crash of music proclaimed the find, and brought him up in his stride. Soon the white-and-tan heads of the leading hounds showed as they rounded the point. One glance he gave them – only one: then his eyes were all for the otter. Whilst he watched the water well in front of the pack, the otter rose, shook his head, rested until his pursuers were within a few yards of him, and dived, showing his back and rudder. 'Takin' things quietly, are 'ee?' said the harbourer in high glee; and then, presently, on observing the hounds lick up the scent as they swam. 'They're tonguing the ream brave.' Scarcely were the words out of his mouth, when up came the otter within a few yards of him. The excited ' Tally ho!' with which he greeted him made the welkin ring.

The squire would always have it that he heard the penetrating scream; but however that may be, it was a good half-hour before he appeared on the summit, and by that time the otter had given the pack the slip and set the harbourer wondering what had become of it. He was amongst the reeds and hidden by the rocks when the squire came up near the overflow, but his cries, as he cheered the pack, betrayed his whereabouts, and presently the squire hailed him across the tarn: 'Have you viewed the otter, my man?' 'Iss, sir, over and over again, but he's creapt away some-wheere out of mark.' The hounds raised their heads on hearing their master's voice, and when he sang out, 'Seek him, my lads! wind him, my lads!' they bustled about, searching along the foot of the cliff as if they meant to find; and very soon they did find, but in a place where neither hounds nor terrier could reach the quarry. The doctor, who was nearest, at once made his way to the spot where the hounds were clamouring and, lying flat on the ledge, succeeded in dislodging the game from its retreat by means of the pole he carried. Thus driven from his only refuge, the otter got no rest. As a good scent guided the hounds, the hunted creature's only chance lay in wearying out his pursuers. And what endurance he showed! He dived hither and thither for over three hours and never landed once; but all in vain, the pack showed no signs of tiring.

At last, in desperation, he slipped over the fall into the pool below and passed down the stream, searching for a hiding-place as he went. Soon he reached the boulder from which the harbourer had watched the hounds and, sighting the crevice at its base, swam through the narrow opening to the hollowed space within. Scarcely was he ensconced when he heard the cry of his pursuers, and a minute later the maddened creatures were roaring at the mouth of his retreat. Squire and followers came tearing down the hill, and when the whipper-in had succeeded in calling off the hounds, Venom, the terrier, was sent in to drive the otter out. 'He'll soon have un out,' said a man in a blue guernsey who knew his worth. But hard and game as the terrier was, the otter was his match. So the squire must have thought, for he determined to send Vic to his assistance. As soon as she was released, the eager little thing swam whining along the passage and joined in the fight; but, owing to the cramped quarters, instead of assisting her mate she hampered him. Once the tip of the otter's rudder showed momentarily, raising the excitement to fever-pitch; but this was followed by a long spell during which not a hair of either terrier or otter was visible.

'They'll never drive un, squire,' the woodman ventured to say. 'Why not flood the varmint out? Theere's a good head of water.'

'Too good a head, I fear; but we'll try. The terriers have had about enough. Get 'em out if you can.'

Watching his opportunity, the woodman managed to pull Vic out almost at once, and Venom after a while. Both were terribly cut up. The sight of their wounds angered the squire, who at once called out: 'Now, men, build a dam, and look lively; that otter shan't live another hour.' All set to work. Except the whipper-in, who had as much as he could do to look after the hounds, every man lent a hand. Some brought big stones, others armfuls of heather, others stone-crop stripped from the rocks, whilst Geordie the gipsy, the parson, the miller and the water-bailiff constructed the dam. Under their eager hands the wall rose steadily across the tail of the pool, and before long the impounded stream began to creep inch by inch up the face of the rock. In half an hour the mouth of the holt was covered; soon, too, the stone which had provided a resting place for the otter; so that he now was compelled to plant his fore-feet against the wall to keep his head above water. Still the water rose, and but for the presence of the imprisoned air the hollow would have been filled and the beast forced to leave and meet its fate in the open. Yet, contracted though the space became, there was a small interval between the water and the roof, and there the otter's nostrils still found relief. Meanwhile the men at the dam had all they could do to hold the stream back; and presently, despite their frantic efforts, the obstruction gave way, and the whole mass rushed roaring down the hill.

'Don't much matter, squire; the otter's drownded before this.'

'May be; but will you put your hand in and draw him out?'

'No, thank 'ee,' replied the miller amidst the loud laughter of the crowd. 'Geordie's the man for that job.'

'I don't mind trying, sir,' said the gipsy, who unhesitatingly approached the rock, knelt in the water, put in his hand to the full length of his arm, and began feeling blindly about the inside. He had worked round three sides and reached the corner to the right when the otter gripped him by the ball of the thumb. His face, which was half turned to the onlookers, must have betrayed the pain he felt, for the woodman called out: 'Have 'ee got un, Geordie?'

'I don't know about that,' replied Geordie, 'but he's got me.'

Slowly he drew the resisting creature towards the aperture, but on being brought to the light it let go, and allowed the man to rise to his feet.

'Rather a nasty wound, Geordie,' said the squire, putting half a sovereign in the bleeding palm.

'Thank you, sir; 'tes only a scratch to some I've had. I'll have another try if you like, sir.'

'No, no, my man, not on any account. The otter deserves his life. We'll leave him for another season, and I hope we may meet again.'

Little did he dream that the game beast which had baffled his best efforts was to become the talk of the country-side, and would for many a day disappoint his hopes and flout his plans.

CHAPTER EIGHT

THE OTTER AND HIS MATE

ᴥ

RATHER MORE THAN A YEAR has passed since the hunt. The vegetation then in flower, after blooming again, has lost its glory, and is now withering and dying. In the marsh the reeds are sapless, the flags stained by decay, the tall-stemmed flowering plants shrivelled to skeletons, disarray and discoloration appear everywhere, save perhaps in the velvet spikes of the mace-reed, whose hue yet rivals in its rich umber the pelt of the otter curled up below them on the spot where he lay in the days of rebellious cubhood. But what a huge fellow he has grown! Fine whelp though he was, he has developed beyond all promise, and there is not an otter on his rounds that can compare with him. He is inches longer and pounds heavier even than his father, and it is little wonder that he should have attracted the notice of sportsmen and become the talk of the country-side. For though since he reached his prime no one has caught more than a glimpse of him, yet keeper, bailiff and moorman have all come on his foot-prints and given such reports of their size that interest has become widespread and people have flocked from far and near to the meets in the hope of seeing him found and hunted.

No one was more interested than the squire, but he succeeded in concealing the excitement he felt, unless, perhaps, it showed in his very caustic language to the field at the least tendency to press the hounds; and when the season ended without the otter being accounted for, no one save his wife and the old butler knew his disappointment. But disappointed he was; and indeed it was almost inexplicable that the hounds should not have chanced on the otter, for he kept to the usual trails and kennelled in the well-known holts. Once they followed his line to the creek, but there, owing to the rising tide, the pursuit had to be abandoned. At another time they actually drew over him where he lay far in under the bank out of mark.

Yet if he bore a charmed life to hunter and hound, he was not fortunate enough to keep quite clear of the other perils that beset him. After having long avoided traps set here and there on his path, he was caught when about fourteen months old by a gin laid in a shallow, and he carried the cruel engine about with him for three days before the chain became so entangled in an alder-root that he was able to wrench himself free. Soon after he was shot at by old Ikey, the wild-fowler, in the channel connecting the Big and the Little Liddens. His quickness in diving at the flash alone saved him, for the man was a dead shot. One night he came on a gang of poachers 'burning the reed' in the pool below the morass, and stood to watch them, fascinated by the flare that lit up the excited faces bending over the water. But though scared by the sight of his enemies, he went only a short distance out of his way to avoid them, and soon after was chasing a salmon in Moor Pool, killing in time to make a hurried meal and reach the tarn before dawn.

Long, arduous and generally vain was his pursuit of the fresh-run fish; but, mighty hunter that he was, he was successful now and then, and enjoyed a hard-earned feast.

It was after such an achievement that the bailiff stood a-stare at his tracks, and shouted to the miller to come down to him. 'What do 'ee think of it?' he asked. 'Think of it?' said the miller, who had noticed only the remains of the otter's banquet, 'think of it? You didn't holloa like that for an old fish, did 'ee? I thought somebody was drow—' Before he could finish the word he saw and, understanding, added in a changed tone: 'Well, well, they prents beat all I ever did see. I'd give a sack of bests to clap eyes on the varmint as left 'em. Where's a lyin', wonder. Anywheres handy, do 'ee think?'

'It's a safe offer you're making, William Richard. You'll nae see the canny vagabond the day. He's no couching near the kill, I'm thinking, but miles and miles awa' – at Lone Tarrn, maybe, or by the Leeddens. That print' – and he pointed to a footmark half in and half out of the water – 'seems to say he was travelling up-water.'

The bailiff was right in supposing that the otter had sought a distant couch, but wrong as to the direction it took and its whereabouts. At that moment the animal was curled up asleep in Rundle's oak coppice overhanging the estuary, ten miles away as the river winds. The next day he was in the bat-cave, but he had not come to stay. At night he was off again, nor did he arrest his steps save to fish and call along the lonely reaches which led to the swamp he was bound for, a good league beyond the bridge. Indeed, he was always on the move, seeming to think it unsafe to sleep two successive days in the same hover. In one fastness, however, he was content to linger – the headland between the Gull Rock and the Shark's Fin. There he would stay for days together, held by the drear solitude, the supply of fish, and the snug lying in the caves that honey-combed the cliff, where man never came, and where, whether the wind blew from the east or from the west, the otter, who disliked exposure to it as much as any fox, could always find a recess on the lee side to shelter in. He took no notice of the tolling of the bell that marked the reef on which he often landed, and the only thing that drove him away was the flooding of his hovers by tempestuous seas. This at last made him seek the drain in the island of the squire's pond the day before he came to the marsh, sharing it with two other dog-otters, refugees like himself. At dusk he foraged along-shore despite the heavy ground seas, and at peep of day returned to his old couch at the foot of the reeds.

To see him lying there no one would dream that he lived in fear of his life. His breathing is placid, his limbs are quiet; no whimper, telling of disturbing dreams, escapes his lips; the very lapdog on the hearth might be more troubled than he. Nor does he seem to be the ferocious beast he is till he raises his head and peers suspiciously through the stems; then the fierce, restless eyes proclaim him a savage and an outlaw as he scans bar and cliff and creek. On the bare patch on the hillside his glance rests a moment – one would say the removal of the furze was a matter of concern to him; but soon, apparently satisfied, he falls to grooming the glossy coat which is his pride. He bestows much care on the massive forelimbs and on the huge, splayed feet whose prints have stirred the imagination of the neighbourhood. A bit of fur on his grey waistcoat not being all he would have it, he licks it again and again; and so the afternoon passes, till the starlings come flying in to roost, the shadows creep over the furze, and the mists gather on the mere.

When night had quite closed in, he rose, slipped into the water and, coming up a good gunshot away, swam rapidly towards the beach. In the shallows he turned his mask as if to make sure the mist harboured no enemy, and then took across the bar, spurning the pebbles and seaweed as he ran. At the edge of the tide he looked back again, but as nothing met his eyes save the ridge and the stars that shone above it, he moved leisurely down the shelving strand, plunged into the curl of the wave, came up in the rough water beyond, made straight for the fishing-ground some two furlongs from the shore, dived, and began scouring the sand and the rocks that chequered it. He looked more like a conger than a beast of prey; yet the fish were quick to recognize their dreaded enemy, and darted from his path. Of sand-eels and flat-fish he took no heed, but gave chase to a bass, pursuing it till it was lost to sight in the depths beyond; then, his lungs being exhausted, he shot up through the seven fathoms of water and lay awhile on the surface, now in the trough, now in the crest of the wave, with his face towards the moon, which had risen clear of the headland. He seemed to be listening, perhaps to the booming in the caves or to the tolling of the bell on the Shark's Fin, but more probably to the surf about the Seal Rock, for presently he swam towards this favourite landing-place. Within a stone's throw of it, however, he dived, and made his way in a spiral down and down until he reached the mouth of a cave in the base of the great pyramid of which the rock is peak.

He knew the place well, for he had been worsted there by a conger some months before, and he had come now in quest of the same fish. His head was scarcely through the weeds that half screened the entrance when he sighted his enemy, who on the instant retreated to its stronghold in the wall of the cave. There, quicker than it takes to tell, each fastened on the other. Matched in weight and strength as they were, it is doubtful whether the otter would have got the mastery even in the open: in the conger's own retreat the attempt was hopeless. But the otter did not realize that, and made frantic efforts to drag the fish from its den. Despite them all he failed to move it a single inch, and the only result of his struggles was to free himself from the conger's jaws. When his breath was all but exhausted he relinquished his hold and turned to go. Thereupon the conger, taking the offensive, made a grab at him; it tried to seize him again near the mouth of the cave to which it pursued him, but in both cases it failed to get a grip of the slippery skin, and the next minute the otter was at the surface.

He had not done with his antagonist. As soon as his lungs were refilled, he dived again, and in a trice was back in the cave, face to face with his enemy, this time with tactics sobered by experience. Instead of laying hold of the fish, he kept making feints at it and retreating, with the object of enticing it into the open; but the wily conger never budged.

Then the otter examined the wall of the cave in the hope of getting at the fish from behind, where the powerful tail gripped the rock. There was no way in, however, and again the baulked marauder had to ascend to take breath. Three times more he made his way down to the mouth of the den, dodging to and fro within a foot of the dull green motionless eyes; but in the end he gave up hope and left.

As he rose to the surface the last time he seized a pollack with such eagerness that his teeth met through it, and this he took to the rock and devoured. Then, swimming towards the shore, he fished along the cliffs, catching wrasse which he left uneaten on the weed-covered ledges where he landed, till at length, tired of wanton destruction, he entered the clitter, and after a long interval came out on the topmost boulder, gained the crest of the cliff, and so crossed to the creek. There he cruised restlessly from bank to bank, raising himself at times half out of the water and looking round as if in search of something. Presently he took to the furze brake that mantles the slope and, traversing the bare patch, passed up the misty valley, only to return to the sand-hills beyond the cottage, where, like an embodied spirit of unrest, he wandered from dune to dune, repeating at times the shrill whistle he had already sounded from the Seal Rock and the bends of the stream that winds along the valley, and standing with raised head pointed now this way, now that, to listen. Once he thought he heard an answering call, but presently discovered his error, and from that moment gave over calling.

Thus he spent the hours of the long night before returning to his lair, where he busied himself in cleansing his lips and whiskers of the slime that adhered to them and smoothing the patches of his coat, disarranged by the conger's jaws. He was long over his toilet, but longer still in falling asleep: the recollection of his defeat kept him awake and caused the hair to rise on his neck as it had risen on the neck of his father at the thought of the pike of Lone Tarn, so that the sun had climbed to half its height before he drowsed and forgot his troubles. Consequently it was late when he bestirred himself and took to the mere, where another dog-otter was already fishing. For a long time each was ignorant of the other's presence, but at last chance brought them together, and as the stranger flashed by, the otter saw that both ears were torn and that he was otherwise scarred by fighting. Later the two animals passed and repassed one another on the surface, and towards dawn, when the otter made for his couch, the new-comer crossed the beach towards the cliffs.

That night the otter, whilst calling from the Seal Rock, heard a rival call from far away across the water in the direction of the Shark's Fin. Later the cry came from the cliffs below Cold Comfort Farm, and close on cockcrow from the clitter where he himself had called an hour before. Every minute he expected the stranger to round the bluff and cross the bar, and presently he saw him come over the pebble ridge and slip into the mere. It was the otter of the night before, who passed down the creek, landed opposite the island, and lay up under the furze.

At nightfall both otters, apparently on good terms, were fishing near the inflow, when the shrill summons of a female reached their ears and set them aflame with passion. They swam as fast as their legs could propel them to the spot whence the call proceeded, and as soon as the otter had landed and licked the face of the skittish little creature awaiting the rivals, he turned to face his enemy. Like two furies they fought in the shallows churned with their incessant movements. As they struggled they got into deeper water, where, locked together, they sank beneath the surface, and so long did they remain immersed that it seemed as though both must be drowned. But the eddies by some decaying lilies told that the fight was still going on, and at last the beasts came up, it might be a yard apart. Quick as lightning they closed again and, rolling over and over, passed from sight a second time in the convulsed water. Then they half rose, and lashing the water with their powerful tails, kept snapping at each other with a viciousness that nothing could exceed, their savage snarls mingling with the clash of their teeth when they failed to get home. For over an hour the conflict raged, now above, now below the surface, till in the end, the old otter, unable to continue the battle, dived to escape further mauling from his victorious foe. But the wild creature's jealousy is never appeased unless its rival is utterly worsted; and a relentless pursuit followed. The bitch otter, now all ears as she had been all eyes, heard the landing, first of the fugitive, then of his enraged pursuer, and soon the crashing of the stems that told of further conflict. At length, in the silence that succeeded the noise of strife, she saw the victor emerge from the mist as he swam towards the spot where she awaited him. Thus, by the discomfiture of the tyrant who had been the terror of every young dog-otter on his rounds, the otter won the little mate who was to share his lot.

Happier than they were, two otters could not be. Their close companionship proved it. Where one was, there was the other. They fished in company, they hovered together, and when they journeyed to fresh fishing-grounds they travelled side by side. A fortnight after they had paired they made their way up the valley of the stream that supplies the mere, and laid up in holts known to the female otter. Three nights' fishing and roaming brought them to the great quagmire where the stream rises, which in summer is but a thread of water winding through the waste of cotton grasses that nod over it. All day they lay asleep on dry couches in the heart of the mire, and at dusk the female led over the high ridge to the watershed that slopes to the northern cliffs where she had been reared. The stream they followed empties itself near a hamlet, and there in the cove under the very windows they fished until daybreak drove them to the cave where they intended to hover. Shaking their coats, they entered – to find an otter already in possession. The instant he raised his mask they saw it was he of the scarred face, but before they advanced a yard he had risen to his feet and was in full flight towards another outlet. The influence of the fight was still on him, and he preferred retreat, even by daylight, to risk of another mauling. They never saw him again.

The otters stayed in the neighbourhood of the hamlet over a week, and during their sojourn nothing disturbed them, nothing even made them prick their ears, except the creaking of the oars as the fishermen rowed past their quarters. On leaving they moved westwards, and beyond two wild headlands came at dawn to the beetling cliffs where the seals have their dwelling in vast caverns hollowed by the Atlantic. Swimming through the turmoil of water at the narrow mouth of the nearest cave, they landed half-way in, climbed to a ledge, from that to another higher still, and there lay down on the bare rock and licked themselves, pausing now and again to look at the seals reclining on the beach of white sand that loomed in the darkness shrouding the inmost part of the cave. When they had completed their toilet they curled up on the smooth slab and, being weary after their long swim, fell asleep, despite the incessant cries of the seals and the ceaseless roar of the waves. They did not awake till the last rays of the sun illuminated the surf at the cave's mouth; but when the shags came flying in to roost, they bestirred themselves, and presently sallied out to fish on the edge of the tide-race and gambol in the swirls of the boiling eddies.

They used the cave for nearly a week, until tempted by the very fine weather to lie out. Then for three days they hovered in the basin at the summit of the Pillar Rock, about a furlong from the cliffs, their presence known only to the gulls and gannets that sailed overhead. On resuming their round, they came, after four hours' journey, to the beach of the Gulf Stream fronting the west, and there they fished and frolicked amongst the waves that broke on the shelly strand, and sought couches amongst the sea-rushes that tuft the dunes. They lingered there week after week till the weather changed, but on the night of a lurid sunset, rounded the grim promontory which marks the end of all the land, and set their faces towards the marsh. On the way thither the female otter kept biting off the rushes and carrying them in her mouth, and when she reached the mere she at once chose a place in the heart of the reed-bed to make a nest. From it soon proceeded the faint squeals of four baby otters, the rearing of which, as it proved, was to try the resources of herself and her mate to the utmost.

CHAPTER NINE

FROST AND FAMINE

ᴥ

AFTER THE NIGHT ON WHICH the whelps were born the
otter repaired to his old hover on the point, whence he
could slip into the water by day and, without exposing
himself, catch what fish his mate needed to make good the drain
on her strength. In going to and from the spot near the nest where
he left his takings for her he soon beat a path amongst the reeds,
by which the little mother reached the mere at nightfall and joined
her mate in raiding the fish that seemed more abundant than ever.
Eels indeed were scarce since the autumn migration, but of pike,
tench and bream there was great store. On these the otters fed for
the most part; but occasionally they fished in the sea, and took toll
of the pollack, plaice, conger and shell-fish found in the inshore
waters. They could not have wished for greater variety of prey, and
the supply seemed as assured as it was inexhaustible.

But there was soon to steal upon the unsuspecting creatures a
frost which exceeded in severity any visitation of cold that even
the old marshman had witnessed. It set in whilst the cubs were yet
blind, and on the second night the water near the nest was frozen
thick enough to bear the otter's weight, as were also the shallows
near the bar, for he landed on the ice there to eat his supper. Before
many days passed, strings of wild-fowl arrived, causing great
rejoicing to the otters, who, far from regarding them as harbingers

of famine, foresaw an agreeable change in their fish diet. Nor had they occasion to look with apprehension on the gradual encroachment of the ice, inasmuch as the breathing holes which they made and kept open enabled them to range as freely as before the frost. Of course, they had to bring their prey to the open water; but for the trouble this gave them they found some compensation in the convenient landing-place afforded by the edge of the ice, which was soon dotted with the remains of their repasts. Moreover, the great sheet of ice served them as a playground when they were weary of gambolling in the mere, and on it they cut mad capers which held the mallard, widgeon, and teal at gaze.

Protected by their thick coats the creatures enjoyed the biting cold, and the cubs, cuddled together in the cosy nest, suffered no ill effects from its rigour. The pike, like the otters, revelled in the frost; but the tench, and the eels that had not gone to sea, felt its pinch, and the bream forsook their usual feeding-grounds. Where these gregarious fish had betaken themselves the otters never knew, but the eels and tench buried themselves in the mud and gave much trouble in the capture. Still, disagreeable though the process was, both these fish were to be had by patient searching in the ooze – at least, it was so at first; then the ground ice, which had gripped the stems of the weeds, spread and spread as the cold increased, until it formed an impenetrable layer over most of the bed of the mere. This followed on the withdrawal of the sea-fish to warmer depths of the offing, inaccessible to the otters, which were thus caused no little uneasiness.

It was the closing of the breathing-holes however a few days later that seriously alarmed them, all but costing the dog-otter his life; for, never dreaming that he would be unable to reopen them at will as heretofore and get the air he needed, he made without misgiving for the best hunting-ground, far in beneath the ice-field, and after capturing a pike, swam unconcernedly to the nearest vent-hole. A single bump of his head, hitherto sufficient, failing to break the crust, he delivered two more blows in quick succession; and when these proved of no effect, he saw his danger, and hurried to the next vent-hole, hard by a frozen-in trimmer. One blow, and only one, did he give; then he dropped the pike, and with lightening-like strokes of his powerful hind-legs made for the open water. It was a race for his life, and he knew it. His lungs ached for want of air; again and again in the next few seconds – seconds that seemed hours – he was on the point of opening his mouth and throat to find an impossible relief, but he forbore, holding on his desperate way, till presently he shot from under the ice-roof and drew breath again in the frosty air. He had escaped drowning, but only to be confronted the very next night with difficulties even more aggravated.

The cold had then reached its greatest intensity. The marsh-man was conscious of its severity as he sat by the fire, listening to the honking of the geese and the trumpeting of the swans – rare sounds, that were music to the aged wild-fowler, and kept him to the chimney-corner later than his wont. Yet at daybreak he was at his lattice to get a view of the overnight arrivals. To his amazement, not a living thing could he see. He rubbed the pane, he rubbed his eyes, and looked again; then he realized – what he had never seen before – that the mere was completely frozen. Despite the depth of the water, the current, and the restless movements of the wild-fowl, the frost had had its way; the vast sheet was one continuous field of steel-blue ice. The otters had witnessed the sealing of the mere, had watched the ducks, geese and swans take wind and melt into the night, before they realized their desperate situation; then, had the cubs been able to travel, they would at once have turned their back on the marshland, as the wild-fowl had done, and made across country for the salmon river, where fish crowded the spawning-beds. But as yet the cubs could only sprawl, and to carry them over the miles of moorland that lay between or to attempt to reach it by way of the sea and the estuary was out of the question; they had no choice but to stay and face the famine that threatened.

As yet they had not suffered at all; indeed, they had caught more fish than they needed, and for their leavings the hill-foxes regularly visited the ice. Amongst them was a poor, half-starved vixen, who, along with the otters, witnessed the ice meet across the strait of open water. Thin as she was, her lot was preferable to that of the otter, with cubs wholly dependant on her; for it seemed impossible to support them unless the frost should soon relent.

Shut off from the mere and the stream that fed it, the night after the closing of the ice the otters turned to the land and quested wherever cover afforded prospect of finding prey. They threaded the reeds and furze-brake, they drew the two osier-beds and tussocky ground between them, but met with nothing save a few dead starlings, from whose sorry skeletons they turned away, hungry though they were. On the next night the hard-set creatures made their way along the stream until they came to the solitary homestead in the heart of the western moor. There they left the ice, clambered up the high bank, and climbed the farmyard wall to the cart-shed, where, standing on their hind-legs, they examined the crannies in the wall for snails, but found none. Coming out, they skirted the pig-sty, passed between an alder-tree and the lighted window, and just as they rounded the corner of the house, found themselves almost face to face with a white cat. Savage tom though he was, he never thought of fighting. In a twinkling he was in full retreat, with both otters at his heels. The male was the faster, and he pressed the cat very closely across the small garden in front of the house, through a gap in the wall, and along the strip of field at the side. He must have overtaken it before reaching the gate had not the cat suddenly swerved and gained a couple of feet, maintaining the lead until it passed through the hole in the stable door at the upper end of the farmyard. The otter followed. Scarcely were they out of sight when the female otter came up the yard on their scent, and also passed in through the aperture at the foot of the door. A fearful spitting ensued, and immediately the cat reappeared with the male so close behind that his nose all but touched the big fluffed-out brush. At a desperate pace both sped over the frozen dung-heap towards the alder-tree; the cat swarmed up, despite the efforts of the otter to seize it, and from its safe perch amongst the top most branches sat looking down at both otters, from whose nostrils the breath issued like jets of steam. Presently the blazing up of the furze fire within drew the eyes of the otters to the window, and when a shadow fell on the blind they slunk away, followed the rude cart-track to the boundary of the farm, and struck straight across the moor in the direction of the Liddens.

A bitter wind swept the waste, but they held on in the teeth of it, crossed the frozen pools, and headed for the mere. On reaching it the female otter made straight for the nest, where she lay oppressed with the dread of famine, till fatigue had its way and sleep made her deaf to the plaints of her unfed cubs. At dusk she and her mate foraged alongshore and found a few limpets, on which they managed to keep themselves and the whelps from starving until the supply failed. Then the little mother, driven to extremity, dulled the gnawing pangs of hunger with seaweed.

To the famine under which parents and whelps were wasting was presently added the outlawed creature's most treacherous enemy – a fall of snow. It began one morning soon after they had sought their couches, and did not cease until a thick covering lay on the marsh and on the hills about it. That night the otters again foraged along the coast, but nothing passed their lips save a few more limpets and a little water from the runnel which still trickled in the cave behind the clitter. Yet, distressed as they were, they rolled and gambolled on the snow in the heart of the mere, whence the tell-tale trails diverged, ready to betray their where-abouts to the first comer. Some hours later, however, more snow fell, obliterating the tracks, and spreading a coverlet over mother and young where they slumbered in the deep nest. The mother's light sleep was broken by the creaking of the windlass over the well and the quacking of the marshman's ducks, but both sounds, under the muffling effect of the snow, seemed to come from far beyond the cottage. The quacking of the ducks was so tantalizing to the famished creature that she actually left the nest and, with just the arch of her back showing above the snow, stole towards the spot whence the noise proceeded. On and on she forged her way, and actually advanced to within gunshot of the duck-house. Then her courage failed her, and caused her to retreat along the furrow she had made.

She was afoot again at early nightfall, joined her mate and fol-lowed him to the shore. After they had fished far and wide to no purpose she turned to him with a distracted look that meant, 'Whither now?' For answer he shifted his gaze from her face towards the cottage; and when, after some hesitation, he moved towards it, she understood, and took her place at his heels. They passed very near the nest – near enough indeed to catch, despite the loud rustling of the reeds, the plaints of the cubs. On hearing the pitiful cries, the mother, her maternal instincts stirred, quickened her pace in a succession of leaps that gave her the lead, which she maintained until the sight of the cottage brought her to a standstill and her mate to her side; then, with their necks raised like little watch-towers, their keen eyes reconnoitred the enemy's dwelling. Nobody stirred, no light showed; the whistling wind favoured them; all seemed propitious, and they drew near the duck-house. Within a few yards of the door they suddenly halted, turning their heads towards the cottage. But it was a needless alarm; the noise that scared them was only the scraping of the wall by the branch of a medlar-tree. The instant they discovered the cause of their hesitation they stepped forward, and put their noses to the crack at the bottom of the door. The scent of the birds within nearly drove the starving creatures mad. But how were they to get at them? Though only a wooden partition separated them from the savoury prey, it was enough. They never thought of biting through it; to crawl under or dig their way in was impossible, and the aperture at the top seemed out of their reach. Nevertheless, this opening was their only chance of entrance; and frantic were the efforts they made to obtain a hold on the top of the door. More than once the otter all but succeeded; had his claws been long and sharp instead of short and blunted, he would have got a footing and probably an entry. But the door rattled and creaked with their futile attempts, and the noise, with the quacking of the terror-stricken ducks, reached the ears of the marshman as he lay listening to the gale. Old and stiff though he was, it was the work of a moment to jump out of bed, open the lattice, and shout at the top of his voice. At the sound the guilty creatures stole away in the direction of the big osier-bed; yet their lot was so desperate that when they neared the furze-rick the little mother stopped and looked back. Despite her dread of the marshman, she would have returned to the duck-house had her mate been willing; but whilst she stood he kept on, and presently she followed and overtook him. It was with weary steps they plodded forward, hopeless as two otters can be. Whither could they turn? Not to the hills, whence even a polecat had come to the marsh to forage; not to the cliffs nor inshore waters; they knew them only too well. And so with no goal to make for, the luckless creatures passed into the night.

CHAPTER TEN

TRACKED

᠅

DAY HAD SCARCELY BROKEN when the old marshman came bustling out of his cottage to see whether the fox – as he supposed the marauder to be – had carried off any of his ducks. Before he had crossed the little garden, however, he descried the snow-marks on the door and, from their size, judged them to be made by a badger, till his eyes fell on the unmistakable trail outside the gate, which placed the raiders' identity beyond all possible doubt.

'Oters! Lor, whoever would ha' thought it?'

And then, as he remembered that the mere was frozen and the creatures shut off from the water, the expression of surprise changed to one of triumph, and forgetting for a moment his decrepitude, he exultingly exclaimed: 'They're mine – sure as eggs, they're mine!' It was not their destruction that elated him, but the prospect – the almost certain prospect – of securing their pelts, and of adding a sovereign to the dwindling store in the thatch.

Of course, before he could dispose of the skins he must find the otters, and shoot them when found; but what could be easier, he thought, than to track them down with such a trail; and then even he, old and infirm though he was, could hardly fail to hit the long-bodied creatures as they left their couches and floundered through the snow. So easy did the task seem in the first flush of excitement, before the difficulties presented themselves, crowding upon him as if to shake him from his purpose. The bitterness of the wind, the depths of the drifts, the possibility – nay, the probability, of the creatures having sought the cliffs, his own physical debility: all confronted him, but only to be made light of and swept aside before he turned and hobbled back to the cottage, determined at all costs to make the attempt.

On crossing the threshold he went straight to the hearth, his eyes raised to the two guns and a brass blunderbuss that rested on wooden pegs above it. The flintlock was within easy reach; but it was the modern gun he meant to use and, standing on tiptoe, he managed to grasp the hammers and take it down. A little over a year before, when he had put the wonderful piece there, he thought he should never use it again, never dreaming of such an easy chance as that offered by otters on the snowed-up mere.

'Can I hold straight enow, wonder.' 'Iss, sure,' came the complacent answer; 'you can hold straight enow for that.'

Nevertheless, as if conscious that he could not and fearing to put his enfeebled powers to the test, he kept blowing on the barrels, though all the dust had gone, until at last, remembering the dark, snow-laden sky, he raised the stock to his shoulder, shut one eye, and looked along the gun. In his younger days man and weapon might have been molten together in bronze, so steadily could he stand and hold; but now, as he had dreaded, the sight zig-zagged over the pane when he aimed at a starling on the medlar-tree outside.

''Tis no use; couldn't hit a seal, leave alone an oter, with muzzle wobblin' all over the place like that – dear, dear, oh, dear!' and he sank into the corner of the settle.

But as he sat before the furze fire which a girl was tending, warmth came back to his hands, the thought of the golden sovereign quickened his blood, and he resolved to make a second attempt. Rising to his feet, he again raised the gun to his shoulder and, holding his breath, aimed at the bird still bunched up on the swaying branch. As the sight kept fairly true to the mark, confidence returned, the old man's face brightened, and resting the weapon against the table, he set about his preparations. He fetched from a drawer in the dresser powder-flask, shot-pouch, caps and wads; he loaded both barrels, and replaced the ramrod. Then he turned up the collar of his worn velveteen coat, pulled the badger-skin cap over his ears and, telling the child he should not be away long, sallied out with the gun at half-cock under his arm.

The trail led past the frozen-in boat towards the tossing withy-bed, but just before reaching it, swerved unexpectedly, as if the creatures had caught a glimpse of some forager who had fore-stalled them, or had all at once thought it best to make without delay for the farther side of the marsh. Bending his bowed figure as he turned, the old man set his face to the gale and plodded bravely along by the side of the tracks, the snow in places reaching half-way up his leather leggings. The depth of it made him hopeful that the otters had not gone far before lying up; so, as he drew near each bit of cover that offered harbourage, he raised the hammers and held the gun at the ready. He did this again and again, whilst beating the tussocky ground on the farther bank of the stream, where the otters had stayed to quest before crossing the unbroken expanse of snow that stretched to the foot of the hill.

At every stride now he was getting more and more under shelter of the land; every score yards the snow was becoming appreciably deeper and deeper, until at last it lay in a big drift that threatened to bar his way. A break in the embankment, fluted and escalloped by the wind, showed where the otters had tunnelled their way through; and the old man, sanguine as to their near neighbourhood, after blowing on his numbed fingers, tightened his grip on the barrels and determined to follow. As the drift was formidable enough to daunt a younger and a taller man, he twice shrank from committing himself to the smothering mass. But again the thought of the golden sovereign, now as he believed so nearly his, lured him on: he held the gun above his head went at the yielding obstacle, sank in it, disappeared all but hand and gun, fought with it, and at last battled through. Furiously brushing the snow out of his eyes, he looked eagerly to right and to left, thinking the game was afoot and striving to escape; but among the laid reeds that met his gaze no living thing stirred: only the big and the little trails, as plain as under the wall of the duck-house, wound in and out amongst the stems, trending in the direction of the mere. 'No hurry, my beauties; I shall come up wi' 'ee by-and-by;' and snap, snap, went the brittle reeds as he made his slow way through them. He kept looking eagerly ahead as though he expected to catch sight of the game retreating before his noisy advance, but nothing caught his eye save the wing of a moorhen on which some fortunate forager had broken his fast.

Yet though he saw nothing of the otters themselves, he came on evidence in the snow which told him they had not spent the night wholly in wandering. Between the reeds and the creek were the beaten places where they had rolled, and a gunshot farther, the slope down which they had slid. On sighting the slide he stopped, astonished that famine-stricken creatures, as he knew they must be, could waste a moment in gambols. 'Most playsomest critturs on God's eerth,' said he; but at once resumed his murderous errand, now with grave misgivings lest he should presently discover that the otters had kept straight on to the bar and cliffs, and got beyond his reach. He was greatly elated, therefore, on reaching the furzy foreland, to find that his fears were groundless, that the otters, instead of crossing the mouth of the creek, had rounded the point and passed up the inlet; for so he felt sure of coming upon them, and most probably in the nearer of the two likeliest holts towards which, whenever he peeped from under the sheltering peak of his cap, the gleaming eyes were directed. It was the ancient pollard whence he had twice seen an otter steal away as he sculled past the island on which it grew.

'They're theere right enow,' the old man said when he saw the trail turn that way, and raising both hammers to full cock, he went on with a stealth he had not before thought necessary. As he reached the island he lost the tracks under the snow-laden tangle. This he proceeded to beat thoroughly; but as he did not really expect to find the quarry there, presently he ceased trampling, looked towards the hollow trunk where he believed they were, called out, 'Harkin', are 'ee?' crept as close to the bole as he dared, and peeped through the cleft. He was obliged to keep at some little distance to get a fair shot when they bolted; and screw his eyes and crane his neck as he might, it was impossible to distinguish the dark bodies in the gloomy recess. He felt sure however they were there, and it occurred to him he might dislodge them with a snowball. Taking up a cake of snow that bore the impress of his hobnailed soles, he made two balls, which he hurled in quick succession through the opening. The second was scarcely out of his hand before he picked up his gun he had laid down, and stood ready to shoot the animals as they escaped; but still no otter showed. 'Not theere after all, s'pose,' said he; yet he advanced on tiptoe to the tree, kicked it, and jumped back with an agility that showed his expectations were not quite exhausted. Again there was no response: nothing stirred except the snow that fell from the rickety crown. Then he walked up to the tree, and peering through the crack, examined the dusky shell from root to branch to find nothing save an old nest with fish-bones on the ground beside it.

Convinced at last that the otters really were not there, he proceeded to make a cast beyond the island, using the gun to steady him as he crossed some exposed ice to the snow. There the sight of the trail brought home to him his want of prevision, and threw him into a rage.

'Drat my stupid old head, why didn't I ring the eyot afore?' came the quick, hot words. 'Once bit, twice shy,' he growled, and strode from bank to bank in search of a return trail which would prevent his being fooled again. But neither on the open snow nor amongst the reeds was there a sign that the otters had broken back. On regaining the track he advanced along it, confident now that the creatures were lying up at the end of the creek.

'At laist, and worth all the trouble. In pride of pelt they'll be. Take your time mind, aim for the head, and the big un fust.'

The nearer he got to the end of the inlet, the more agitated he became, until, on reaching the spot where the otters had passed in single file between two tussocks before entering the brambles, he was in a fever of agitation. But despite his excitement, the precautions he took showed he had got himself well in hand, that he was anxious to make the most of his hardly earned chance. He raised the flaps of his cap that no sound might escape his ears; he brushed away every particle of snow from the barrels of the gun, and to satisfy himself that the weapon would not misfire, he raised the copper caps and saw that the powder was still up in the nipples.

Then, everything being ready, he began to trample upon the matted sprays in order to drive the otters from their last possible retreat.

He had taken some half a dozen steps when a patch of snow falling from the brambles well in front informed him that something was afoot. On the instant he stopped to listen, whilst his restless eyes sought the likely points of escape, and the gun shook in his nervous hands. As the otters did not show, he felt sure they were stealing away before him, and carefully watched some reeds into which they must pass on leaving the thicket. Seeing a slight agitation in the stems, he tore like a madman through the rest of the scrub, and stood at the edge ready to shoot. But, too excited to await the otter's pleasure, after the briefest delay he advanced again, not however with the reckless strides of a few moments before, but with gingerly tread, as if now that the supreme moment had come he was apprehensive of dislodging the creatures he was so eager to kill. He had taken a few cautious steps when there was a slight rustling; then, to his dismay, a bittern rose and flew down the creek. Up went the gun, the fore-finger found, but did not pull, the trigger; and the bird escaped without further scare. It was a terrible disappointment, under which the old man collapsed. The gun fell from his shoulder; his jaw dropped; the eyes, but an instant before full of fire, were dull and listless. He seemed inches shorter as he staggered through the reeds and along the gully towards a small enclosure about which the banks rose almost sheer.

'Niver can be in the Piskies' Parlour to be sure; and yet how could they get out?'

The words were scarcely out of his mouth when his eyes fell on the fresh marks against the face of the scarp. Then he saw the foot-prints left on the snow by the otters as they sprang to the lowest ledge.

'Has the frost touched my brain, or the little folks my eyes? Nonsense! nothin' of the kind; thee'rt seein' things as they are. Well, well,' he went on after drawing a long breath, 'I've been wanderin' about the ma'sh for wellnigh fifty year, and come on many tracks, but never prents like these. Lor mercy! must be a mighty big varmint as left 'em. What a catch if only I could ha' bagged un!'

The sight of the footprints had put fresh life into him; he determined to follow as far as he could.

'I'm bone-tired, but I'll see it through if I drop on the track.'

Only a cat could follow where the otters had climbed; so he made his way back to the creek and clambered up the high bank to the wind swept ridge leading to the cliffs. A forlorn figure the old man looked as he fought his way in the teeth of the gale to the brink of the precipice, only to find the trail end on a slab of rock, from which the spray had washed some of the snow that covered it.

'It's all up,' he said, turning his eyes to the great pile of loose rocks farther along the cliff; 'they're gone to clitter. Now, old fool, goest home along.'

After a glance at the sea, on which not a sail or a wing showed, he made his way to the point of the bluff above the mere, and letting himself carefully over the edge, succeeded by clinging to rock and tussock in making the descent without mishap. At the foot he stood awhile to rest; then, presently, set out across the snowfield for the cottage, his thoughts full of the otter, which however he had given up all hope of getting.

So convinced was he that the creatures were in the cliff that he attached no importance to the trail he stumbled on in the midst of the mere, till he came to the spot where the tracks forked; but there he awoke to the significance of the situation. 'Oh, oh,' said he, as he checked his steps, 'so this was where you parted, was it? – one for the reed-bed, t'other for up along, the withies most like.'

After a pause he added with a chuckle, 'Jack oter, you're mine yet.'

At the thought of the valuable prize falling to him he was all life and energy again: the vigour of his stride showed it as he stepped along the furrow made by the otter, with eyes fixed on the isolated clump near the inflow through which he expected it would pass. His surprise and excitement may be imagined when on reaching it and ringing it, he found no sign of track on the snow beyond.

'Niver can be in this morsel of a patch,' said he under his breath, as he took up a station between it and the reed-bed he felt sure the otter would make for. 'Yet eh must be, eh must be.' Then, raising his voice, he called out, 'King Oter, thy time is come; show thyself and get the business over.' With that he began to beat the reeds with the gun, trampling the stems as he advanced. In the midst of the clump he came on the couch. He stooped quickly and felt that it was warm. 'I knawed thee was theere,' said he; and crack, crack, crack went the reeds as he levelled them with the ground.

Less than a dozen yards of cover remained when the old man, in his anxiety to get a glimpse of the otter, knelt down and peeped through the stems. Only the head of the otter showed, but the eyes of man and beast met. Before the marshman could regain his feet, the creature had bolted, making wild leaps in its attempt to escape. Bang! Bang! first one barrel, then the other; and the old man, who believed he had wounded the animal, started in mad pursuit. For a few strides he actually gained on the short-legged creature: but for want of breath he might have overtaken it. As it was, all he could do after covering a score yards was to lament his helplessness, and watch the huge dark form draw farther and farther away. 'What a grand beast!' he gasped again and again; then suddenly, 'He's down!' he exclaimed, starting to run. But the otter was not down: not a pellet had struck him: he was only lost to sight in a drift. When he reappeared near the bar, the excited marshman saw his error, and once more stood to watch. On reaching the ridge the otter ran along it, showing his magnificent proportions. Once he stopped to look back at his enemy; a few moments later he disappeared from view, and the old man turned on his heel and made for home.

CHAPTER ELEVEN

BACK IN THE OLD HAUNTS

O N PASSING OUT OF THE OLD man's sight the otter made for the cliffs, where he lay close, impatiently awaiting nightfall that he might return to his mate. The light had scarcely faded when he took to the water. Early though it was to be abroad, he had not got far before he espied her swimming towards him, and presently he saw that she held a cub in her mouth. The reports of the gun had made her apprehensive for the safety of her young, the tiniest of which she was removing first to the clitter. The sea was rough and the spindrift blinding, yet she held on with her precious burden till she had reached a cave behind the boulders and laid the dripping mite in a nest there. Then she hurried back for another; when that was placed beside the first she fetched another, and yet another, till all four were in safety.

As soon as she had deposited the last she assisted her mate to scour the sea-bed between the cliffs and the Seal Rock in search of prey to relieve her maddening hunger. For hours the couple drew likely ground without result; but when they were about to end their quest they came on a stray pot containing a big crayfish. The find was as welcome as it was unexpected. In their eagerness to get at the prize the starving creatures swarmed about the osier cage like terriers about a rat-trap, vainly striving to find a way between the bars or through the aperture at the top, which was all but closed by the battering the pot had received. It was a most tantalizing situation. The otters' only hope was to stay near the cage until tide and ground-swell should drive it ashore, dash it to pieces against the cliff, and leave the crayfish at their mercy. So through the long night they never left it except to breathe. In the end their patience was rewarded. The breakers got hold of the trap, tumbled it over and over, and wedged it between two rocks, smashing one of the bars, and making a hole through which the female otter managed to squeeze. In a twinkling she had seized the fish and crushed its life out. As soon as the wave which had covered her withdrew, she began devouring her prey. Whilst she feasted, the otter made frantic efforts to get in, but failed, and presently desisted, contenting himself with the bits that escaped through the bars. The tide rose, yet the little creature, despite the rush of the waters and the blows she received from the stone that weighted the pot, remained where she was until she had consumed all except the feelers and harder parts of the shell; then, leaving by the way she had entered, she skirted reef and ledge in the dawn-light, and made straight for the clitter. Her one thought was for her famished cubs, which, before the sun was very high, she was suckling from her abundance, purring whilst they fed.

That day a thaw set in, and a shag appeared on the Seal Rock. The otter, who had shifted his quarters to avoid the drippings from the cliffs, after watching the bird's fishing for a time, began himself to fish. At the end of a long, fruitless quest he landed; but now, in his extremity, no longer careful for his safety, he lay out in the open on a granite boulder. Happily no harm came of it. Through the night he and his mate hunted in the deep water beyond the rock, still without seeing a fin, so that when the sun peeped above the sea the creatures returned to the cliffs in despair. At noon the mother brought her puny little ones from the dank cave and laid them in the sun's rays to enjoy the genial warmth; but as they soon cried to be fed, for fear their plaints might betray them she carried them back to the nest, and there, lulled by the sob of the restless tide, she at length dropped off to sleep.

She might have slept for two hours when the clamour of sea-fowl awakened her and brought her in haste to the edge of the clitter, where the otter was already on his feet gazing at a flock of gulls, whose excited movements showed they were over fish. Whilst they looked the shoal disappeared, and the gulls dispersed – like the wonderful scouts they are – to watch for its return to the surface. The instant the birds congregated over an agitated patch of water between the clitter and the Seal Rock the eager otters slipped into the sea. Soon they were near enough to distinguish the silvery spoil in the beaks of the birds, and two minutes later they were in the middle of the shoal.

Luckily the fish were sprats, so small that the otters could eat them without landing, and if the shoal had remained long on the surface the animals would have filled themselves to repletion; but before they had gobbled down a tithe of what they needed the fish again sought the depths. The otters pursued as far as breath allowed, raising themselves in the water when they came up, to look towards the direction the fish had taken. Time after time they stood up to gaze over the heaving surface, but with the gathering of the dusk and the withdrawal of the gulls to the cliffs they ceased, and landed on the Seal Rock.

As the few sprats had excited rather than allayed their

appetite, after a short rest they began to fish again, little dreaming of the struggle in which they were almost at once to be engaged. For they had scarcely reached the bottom when a tiny fish darted across an opening between two clumps of weeds; close behind, in pursuit of it, came a big conger. At once they took up the chase of the pursuer where it followed its prey from tangle to rock and from rock to tangle and presently, when a sudden turn brought them within striking distance of the unsuspecting fish, they rose from beneath, careening over so as to fasten on the fleshy throat. Their teeth had scarcely met before the still depths were convulsed by the writhings of the fish in its efforts to shake off its assailants, who however hung on till their victim grew quieter. Then, using their tails and hind-feet, they raised their prey through fathom after fathom until, for lack of breath, they had to let go and come to the top. It was a few seconds only before they were back again; but the disabled fish made good use of the interval, and had reached the mouth of the cave when they overhauled it. They began anew to drag it towards the surface. The monster writhed in their grip, trying again and again to fold its tail about some projecting rock past which it was being lifted, but it failed to get a hold, and was borne up, and up, and up, until the stars were just visible through the water. Then the otters were again compelled to let go and rise to breathe. At the third attempt they barely held their own against the fish, so violent was its resistance; at the next, however, after a terrible struggle they succeeded in getting it to the surface, where with glowing eyes they lay and rested beside their ghostlike prey before essaying to land it. Soon they began towing it to the cliffs towards which the tide had drifted them, but before they had got far the conger, singling out the stronger enemy, strove to coil itself about the otter. Failing to get a grip of the slippery, lissom form, it lashed the sea as if to vent its rage at its own impotence. Then it took to shaking its head and snapping its jaws. The otters however had it helpless, and held grimly on their way till they brought it to the edge of the breakers, where from sheer exhaustion they let go, resting awhile to recover a little strength before committing themselves to the welter of the surf. Though the fish too seemed to be at its last gasp, suddenly, as if roused by the warning voice of the breakers to a final effort, it shook itself free from the otters, who had seized it as it stirred, and with a great swirl, disappeared beneath the surface. Like a flash the otters were after it, but rose with out it once and again. The third time the fish was between them. Almost immediately a wave bigger than its fellows curled over them, buried them in its mass of waters, and hurled them on the sand, up which the otters dragged their prize inch by inch till they had brought it to a wide table of rock beyond reach of the surf. Although out of the water, the conger still writhed until the otter bit through its great backbone; then it lay almost quiet whilst the starving creatures sliced and munched and gulped as if they never would be satisfied. Satiety however came at last, and when they could eat no more they with drew to the clitter – night though it was – to sleep off the orgy that marked the close of the days of want.

With the continuance of mild weather pollack and plaice returned to the inshore waters, so that soon, through the plentiful supply of food, the otters regained their good condition, whilst the cubs lost their emaciated appearance and throve apace. From that time the ties that bound the otter to his mate grew looser and looser, and a week after the young had learnt to swim he left her altogether, to resume his solitary life.

For a while he kept to the headland and the cliffs near the Gull Rock: then, tiring of these haunts, he crossed to the wild coast opposite, where he lingered week after week, until the breath of spring quickened his roving instincts and set him longing for the old trails. So he retraced his steps from the point of the promontory to which he had penetrated, and on the night of the full moon drifted up the estuary to Tide End. There, after fishing, he sought the shelter of a pile of faggots before the villagers were astir. He slept soundly, despite the near neighbourhood of man, and when dusk fell swam past the lighted cottages towards the wood. Landing there and striking straight through the trees, he held on without a stop till he reached the rude wall at the upper end, on which he stood to listen to the croakings proceeding from the marshy flat beyond. Presently he stole towards the biggest of the pools that silvered the rushy waste; but when about midway he must have been heard or seen, for the frogs there ceased their chorus, and forthwith the marsh became as silent as when in the grip of the frost. On gaining the water's edge he dived, and in a twinkling was back with a frog, which he skinned and devoured. This was the first of some half a score that he caught and ate before repairing to a ditch-like piece of water, dark from the shadowing alders, where he long remained feasting. At length he had had enough and, leaving the marsh, made for the river, which he followed mile after mile till he reached the morass and laid up in the hollow bank in which he was born.

Meanwhile otter-hunting had begun, and all the country-side over men were on the lookout for his tracks. Not since the mysterious disappearance of the bob-tailed fox had so keen an interest been taken in any wild creature. Through the winter he had been the topic of conversation in the chimney-corner of cotter and crofter, and a very frequent intruder on the thoughts of the squire. The slightest association was enough to recall the creature to his mind: the sound of running water, the appearance of a salmon-poacher in court, even the sight of the short-legged animal carved on the screen of the parish church – indeed, his preoccupation showed itself in many acts of his daily life.

Whilst the snow lasted he went every morning to the pond to look for tracks, and as soon as the first daffodils bloomed he began to dip his hand in the streams to try their temperature, longing for the time when the water would be warm enough for the hounds to draw them. In the meantime he busied himself with the various duties of a master of otter hounds. He visited the kennels every day to make sure that the hounds got road exercise to harden their feet. He succeeded after much trouble in inducing the keepers on neighbouring estates to remove the traps which had been the bane of the Hunt. A fortnight before the opening meet he rode round to see the water-bailiff, the miller, the moorman, old Ikey, and the marshman, asked them to keep a lookout for the otter, and parted from each of them with the words, 'Now don't forget, my man. Morning, noon, or night, bring me word if you strike his trail.' It is not true, as alleged by the gossips of the port, that he offered a reward of ten pounds for information that should lead to the finding and death of the otter, though had there been an offer of twice that sum the trackers could not have shown greater keenness than they did. There was evidence of it even before the search began, for every man from far and near who meant to take a part turned up at the hour fixed for the allotment of the waters, determined to get his rights. This unusual procedure had been adopted at the instance of the squire, in order to avoid the disputes and bad blood which he foresaw would arise unless the beats were formally assigned before the season opened.

Raftra, in his 'Annals of our Village,' gives a very full account of the meeting. It took place at the Druid's Arms, with Reuben Gribble, the landlord, in the chair. Between him and the red-bearded water-bailiff sat the venerable tenant of the Home Farm, called in ostensibly on account of his wide knowledge of the streams, but really because of his well-known powers of conciliation, which were needed as soon as the business of the evening began. The chief difficulty was with Sandy, the bailiff, who claimed by virtue of his office the whole length of the river, from Tide End to Lone Tarn. Though he was one against a score, counting the men in the doorway, he seemed bent on maintaining the unreasonable position he had taken up. When the miller and the moorman asked him for the reaches which they preferred and which every man round the table thought they were entitled to, he brushed their requests aside as if they were nobodies. As Raftra says, a Lord High Ranger couldn't have treated vagrom men with more contempt. This haughty demeanour enraged everyone; in fact, it was all Geordie and the wilder spirits could do to keep their clenched fists off the bailiff's person. As it was, angry words passed, but when a fight between the gypsy and the Scot seemed imminent, the old reeve rose, lifted his thin hands to command silence, and said:

'Don't quarrel, my friends – don't quarrel; better the otter never came anist us if it's to lead to blows. And yet, as an old tracker, it does my heart good to see how eager every man of 'ee is to get a good beat. For what else does it mean but this, that the love of sport among us is as strong as ever it was? It makes me long to be one of 'ee, it do; to be young again, abroad at peep o' day, when the sun is touchin' the cairns and the wakin' world is fresh and sweet, to feel once more the joy of comin' on the wild rover's prents. This minit in my mind's eye I can see the five round toe marks and the seal of the otter I spurred beside the Kieve. You've heard of the sport he gave. An old man's tongue will run away with him – run riot, I ought to call it. Your indulgence, my friends, and your further patience while I touch on the matter that brought me to my feet. And let me say by way of preliminary and to all alike, don't be overreachin'; don't, simply to keep others out, claim more water than you can search. "Live and let live" is a good motto for a sportsman, be he Englishman or Scot; and this I'm sure of, that my friend beside me will look at things as a big-minded man always do, and prove himself the good neighbour we've taken him for.

'Mr. Macpherson, we've treated 'ee like one of ourselves since the coach dropped 'ee at the cross roads now three year back; the more so, maybe, since we've got to understand your mouth-speech. True, there was a little soreness because Zachy Kelynack didn't get the job, but only for a month or two; and we did our best to hide it, agreein' among ourselves that if the Duchy slighted our own man, 'twas no fault of yourn, and no case for pitchin' and featherin', or even for the pump. Come to look back upon it, for a rough-and-ready sort of people, whose parish is their world, we met thee hansomely, though I say it, as I hope we shall every strainyer who looks us straight in the eyes and does his duty without fear or favour. Now, is it askin' 'ee too much to show a friendly spirit in return and a little consideration for local feelin'?' Here the speaker paused; but, as the bailiff showed no sign of giving in, he went on: 'Come, come, Sandy, only try and see the matter as we do. William Rechard and Matthew Henry were born and reared upon the moor, and have known the river all their lives. Right or no right, do 'ee wonder they think their-selves entitled to a reach or two? No, you cannot, you do not. Be strong, my friend, and give way.'

Now, it was not so much what the old man said as the way he said it that made the appeal seem irresistible to all but the bailiff. And truly the voice and manner of the speaker, mellow as the rich light that flooded the low-raftered room, would have gone home to men even less emotional than his countrymen; but the dour Scot seemed to be not the least affected till the landlord, who had hur-riedly disappeared through a side-door, returned with a double-handled jug of old cider, and by the influence of the seductive liquid brought him to reason. At the fourth cup he gave in with a good grace, yielding to the miller the three miles of water above the mill. At the sixth he granted the reach above Moor Pool to the moorman, who also got the stream near his cot; old Ikey got the Liddens, as was only fair, since the pools were on his holding; the marshman, the marsh; and the poachers shared the waters that remained, the order of choice being decided by the length of straw, drawn from the landlord's closed hand. Geordie and Tom, who as leaders of their profession had first and second choice, to their cha-grin got the shortest straws.

Now for rivercraft or marshcraft the fourteen men that daily gave at least an hour or two to the search could not, perhaps, have been matched outside that most ancient terrain of the otter-hunter, the Principality of Wales. Yet though the otter followed the usual trails over the moor, the trackers never once came on a sign of him. The reason is not far to seek. The beds of the river and the streams are for the most part rocky, the shallows and landing-places pebbly, and spits of sand are few and far between. It was on these last that the trackers relied to find the foot-prints, and at dawn they might have been seen bending over them, plying their craft as eagerly as men seeking gold or precious stones. They found nothing, for the otter had never set foot there. Once, indeed, he left his tracks within a bowshot of Moor Pool – tracks so plain that they seemed to cry out; but before the bailiff reached the spot the river rose and obliterated them, and the bailiff never knew how near he had been to discovery.

After the quest had gone on for nearly a month, when men and squire were beginning to fear that the otter had abandoned the district or that his skin was adorning the bedroom floor of some keeper who had trapped him, by the merest chance the moorman happened on the prints near the boundary of his little holding. He was struck all of a heap, as he said, at the unexpected sight; but on recovering himself he remembered the squire's words and the look in his eyes, so, though the sun was only a few handbreaths above the moor, he left the peat where he had dropped it and set off at a brisk pace for the Big House. In his excitement he forgot the hounds were out until he reached the wood; but there, to the amazement of the watching woodman, who had wondered at his haste, he suddenly turned, late as it was, and made for the cross-roads, hoping to intercept the squire and save himself a very long journey.

By good luck the moorman reached the top of the hill just in time to hail the squire as he rode by, and ran down breathless to where he had drawn rein.

'Tracked un at laist, squire,' he gasped.

'Good news, Pearce. I've had a long day, but I'll go back with you.'

'It's a brave way off, sir.'

'No matter.'

So leaving the hounds to the whipper-in, he accompanied the man to the moor, and examined the tracks by the light of the lantern the moor-man had fetched from his cottage.

'They're his, right enough, Pearce. Funny place to come on them.'

''Tes and 'tesn't, come to think of it, for I've spurred otters on this very bit of ground more than once before, and all goin' the same way. 'Tes a line of traffic from the strame to the revur.'

'Ah, that's interesting. But, my word, what amazing prints they are! What weight do you put him at?'

'Afeerd to say, sir.'

'They're a couple of days old, Pearce.'

'Iss, sir, all that, but you mind what you told me.'

'All right, my man. I attach no blame; that's not my meaning.'

'He's alive and in the country, sir.'

'Yes, yes; to be sure he's in the country. Great thing to know that. It will hearten every man of us. Great day, red-letter day when we drop on him, eh, Pearce?'

Then he rose to his feet, but was almost immediately on his knees again for a last look. At length he tore himself away, slipped a crown-piece into the moorman's hand, remounted, bade the man good-night, and galloped off.

Now the moorman on his way to stop the squire had over-taken and told the post-woman: the blacksmith at the cross-roads had overheard what he said; and from these two the news spread so rapidly and so far that before the morrow's sundown it was known through the country-side that the otter had been tracked on Matthew Henry's splosh, that the squire had gone there and seen the prints with his own eyes. To what a pitch of excitement the trackers were aroused by the tidings may be imagined. Most of them were at the stream-side at the first glimmer of day, and all of them remained out hours longer than usual. The squire, expecting that word of the otter might be brought at any moment, feared to leave the house. He had even given orders that Limpetty, the whipper-in, was to have his meals at the kennels and to sleep in the loft.

But the otter's plans ran counter to the hopes and expectations of his enemies. On the third day after the discovery of his tracks he forsook the moorland for the creek, where he feasted on mussels and flounders till he tired of them. Then he made down the estuary to the headland; he robbed the trammels and spillers of the choicest fish, and on one occasion actually took a bass off a whiffing-line.

Thus another month passed, by the end of which the trackers who had stood so high in the estimation of their neighbours began to be made slight of, and even to be laughed at. Right welcome to them were the heavy rains that rendered river and streams unfit for hunting and furnished a sound excuse for discontinuing the hopeless quest. The flood was indeed a big one, as the mark on the door of the miller's stable testifies. To this day the old man at the port will tell you they never before knew the sea stained to such a distance by the peaty water, adding in the same breath that the run of fish was 'a sight to see'.

Harbour and estuary seemed alive as the salmon made their way up the river: people gathered at different spots to see them pass. Villagers crowded the bridge at Tide End where the fish take the weir; Geordie and Tom stood at the fall beneath the pines; the miller, at the foot of his garden, watched them go up the new ladder.

'Bra run, Reuben,' remarked he to the landlord at his side.

'Iss, fy, and good fish among 'em. That's a heavy fish goin'
up now. He'll do it; no, he won't, he an't. That basin is like
Malachi's hen, too high in the instep. I said it was when they were
puttin' un in.'

As the miller took no notice, he bellowed in his ear, 'Custna
hear what I'm sayin', you?'

'Hear! Of course I can; I'm not deef. Hear, indeed! Thee
wust drown the roar of a dozen floods, thee wust! What have 'ee
got to say?'

'Why, only this, that he'll be up afore long.'

'What do 'ee mean by he?'

'What do I mean? What can a man mean these days but
one thing?'

'How teasy you are.'

'Teasy, indeed! Do 'ee wonder at it? That varmint has got on
my nerves. I'm always thinkin' about un, I caan't sleep for'n, and if
I do, I see un in my dreams. Most like he will come up; and I hope
and trust he will, and that the hounds will find and kill un, or
what'll become of the parish I don't know. From the squire to Tom
Burn-the-Reed we're gettin' in a poor way, and you the one man
gettin' any good out of it.'

When the flood began to fall the otter did come up, and the
first night spent hour after hour, to no purpose, chasing salmon in
the pool below the rapids. At dawn he climbed to the ivy-covered
branch of a tree overhanging the river, to sleep as well as his
uncomfortable quarters allowed. That night he killed in the Kieve;
early in the morning the moorman disturbed a pair of buzzards
from the remains of his feast, and tried to cross to look for tracks;
but the current was dangerous, and after being nearly washed off
his feet he turned back.

The river had not yet fallen to hunting level; but as soon as it had, the bailiff, the miller and all the others were out again, confident that the otter was up and, despite previous failures, hopeful that they would come on his track on one of the many new sand-spits left by the receding waters.

CHAPTER TWELVE

THE LONG TRAIL

I T WAS 'BETWIXT THE LIGHTS', as he would have said, when the miller closed the door quietly behind him and made his way among the nut bushes to the ford where his search for the otter usually began. No track marked the ground by the water's edge, nor was there a sign on any of the likely spots all the way to the stranded alder, where he sat to rest awhile before resuming his beat. The pine-tops were then aglow and the birds in full song, but they meant nothing to him in the mood he was in; his thoughts, as his words showed, were all for the otter.

'Not a trace. Pools full of fish, too, and everythin' as keenly as can be. Yet I'm sure he's up, and sartin he'll be spurred afore the day's much older. Wonder who'll be the lucky man?'

At the thought of his rivals he sprang to his feet and soon had reached the precipitous bank above the shelving strand where, though so many landing-places were undisturbed, he had every hope of coming on the tracks. Most carefully the eager eyes examined every foot of sand visible between the rowan-trees as, slowly on hands and knees, the miller advanced towards the bend which commands the likeliest spot of all. There twenty feet below he saw a salmon lying and, with the same glance, marked the tracks beside it. The descent of the scarp was nearly as perilous as the crossing of the current, but he accomplished both without mishap, and a few seconds later was crouching beside the footprints.

'By the life of me they're his, and not many hours old.'

His face, no less than his agitated voice, showed the wild excitement that possessed him as he rose and made down the wood as fast as he could lay foot to ground. When he reached the mill he was almost at his last gasp, but he bridled and mounted the pony, which he urged to a gallop through the open gate and up the stony lane. He was on his way to the squire.

As he rode through the hamlet, where the clatter of the hoofs brought the villagers to door and window, his cries of 'Tracked un!' roused man and boy to a fever of excitement, and sent the sexton in hot haste to the belfry to apprize the country-side. The miller, however, leaving them behind, was soon at the lodge gates. There he nearly frightened old Jenny into hysterics by his shouts; but she took her revenge, for after letting him through she shook the keys in his face and screamed after him, 'Mad as a curley! mad as a curley!' until he rounded the bend where the mansion comes into view. The whole house seemed asleep; but as the miller crossed the bridge over the moat the squire appeared at a window and, in a voice that betrayed the tension of his feelings, called out:

'Where?'

'Longen Pool, sir.'

'Fresh?'

'Last night's.'

'Rouse the men, Hicks; we shall need every hand we can muster.'

Before he had got through the plantation on his way to the kennels the clang of the fire alarm broke on the still morning air, and when he returned from his round, squire, whipper-in and

hounds were making their way through the park with a small ret-
inue of servants in their train. At the hamlet they were joined by
the parson, the parish clerk, the landlord, two sawyers, and six or
seven others, and between the pound and the river by a few
crofters, whom the church bell had summoned from outlying
homesteads.

They crossed the water below the pool, the squire examined
the tracks, the hounds were laid on, and the rocky gorge with all
the wood about it immediately resounded with their wild music,
while the squire and every man behind him thrilled at the
prospect of at last coming up with the creature whose movements
had so long baffled them. The ground was very rough, and in
parts swampy, yet not a man turned back. That active, hard-
conditioned followers made light of the obstacles and the pace
was, of course, not surprising; but that the landlord, the clerk, and
the chef – short-legged, eleven-score men every one of them –
should scramble over rocks and fallen timber, flounder through
thickets and boggy places, and still hold on, bedraggled and
breathless though they were, testified to the fascination the pursuit of the giant otter had for them.

Some two miles above Longen Pool the squire caught sight of
spraints on a boulder in the middle of the river, and knew at once
from their position at its upper end that the otter which had
dropped them was travelling down-water. At once he recalled the
hounds and began drawing anew the reaches he had passed. He
tried every holt he came to, but without result.

'Do you think he's gone down?' shouted the squire to the
miller across the river.

'I don't, sir. I didn't find a trace from the ford up, and, as you
know, the hounds didn't give a sign.'

'Well, there's no holding worth the name between here and Longen. Where can he be?'

The puzzling question was answered by the deep note of Dosmary from an overgrown watercourse that served to drain the morass. No need was there for the squire to cry out, 'Hark to Dosmary'; for the hounds, on hearing the summons they knew so well, flew to her where she threaded the reed-bed before taking the steep leading to the moor. Then up the all but bare face the twenty couple made their way in a long winding line. Close after the hindmost pressed the squire, the parson and five others, all sound of wind and limb, capable of holding on to the end of the promontory, if need be. Not a word passed until the hounds had crossed the stream where it was thought the otter might have laid up, and then only 'Liddens, men,' and 'Ay, sir!' from the moorman in response. Even the sight of the otter's footprints in the next hollow drew no remark; though it caused an unconscious quickening of the step up the long, heathery slope, from whose brow the sea showed beyond the hazy outline of the land. Wide on either hand rose grim piles of rock, where down this avenue of cairns the seven, comrades on many a trail, sped in the wake of the pack towards the Liddens, shimmering in the distance.

But if the seven were elated as never before, there was one on the far side of the moor who was suffering a bitter disappointment. It was the old marshman. He too had discovered the tracks of the otter and, full of his tidings, had driven to the mansion as fast as his Neddy could cover the ground, only to learn from the butler that squire and hounds had already been summoned and gone off to the river. Staggering though the blow was, he bore up till beyond the gates; but on the open moor he broke down, said it was a judgement on him for tracking the varmint in the snow, and let the donkey find the way home as best it could. When they reached the cottage he set the animal loose, tried in vain to shake off his trouble by overhauling the trimmers, and finally sat down on a bench, with his back to the mud wall and his face to the marsh. It was green and gold with the swords and banners of the iris; the air was drowsy with the hum of bees and the sea murmured on the bar; yet the old man noted nothing of it. His thoughts, too, were all of the otter; he was busy trying to reconcile the seemingly contradictory discovery of the tracks in two places so far apart. "Tes a job to piece 'em together with leagues – iss, leagues – of moor between. Why, look here. 'Tes all eight miles from the revur to the Liddens, and a good three as the hern flies from the Liddens to the ma'sh; a long journey, an unaccountable long journey for a crittur that edn framed for travellin'. On a midsummer night, too, and he more afeard of the glim o' day than a cheeld of the dark. And then to turn his back on the salmin for the pike, and they poor as can be from spawnin'. Why, the thing edn in reason. But, theere, what's the use of wastin' breeth when he's done it? For the prents are hisn and none other, and nawthin' could be fresher.'

The marshman was right: the otter had crossed. At star-peep the creature had slipped from his holt in the side-stream and floated down to Moor Pool, where he killed a grilse, took a slice or two from its shoulder, and left it on the pebbles. Thence, contrary to his habit, he passed down-water, throwing the fish into a panic at every pool. Waves in the shallows showed where the most timid fled at his approach; some however remained and here and there, as the water favoured his purpose, he gave chase. Twice the formidable marauder landed with victims which he left uneaten on the bank where he laid them, for lust of slaughter, not hunger or love of pursuit, possessed him, and he was moved by a restlessness greater than he had ever shown. True, he climbed at times on snag and boulder; but that was only for an instant before taking again to the water or bank, as fancy led.

At Longen Pool his coming caused a general exodus, but he singled out one salmon, and by his wily tactics prevented it from fleeing with the others to the rapids below. The long chase which followed was for a while in favour of the fish; yet the otter, who was not to be denied, in the end wearied it out and carried it to the bank, where he bit viciously at the shoulder, as if to wreak his vengeance on the prey that had caused him so much trouble. Presently he re-entered the water, cleansed his blood-stained muzzle, and making upstream turned aside into the wet ditch and traversed the morass.

On gaining the high ground above it he stood awhile, as if asking himself whether at the late hour he might venture across the moor. The instant his mind was made up he set out at a rapid pace, glancing at the keeper's lodge as he went by, and again at the sleeping hamlet before crossing the road and entering on the waste, over which he held on his way till nearly abreast of the cromlech. There he halted whilst he sounded the call and listened. Twice he uttered the shrill cry, his mask turned in the direction of the lone pool to the north; but there was no answer in the mocking whistle of the curfew, so he moved on again under the fading stars, and at last came to the Liddens.

He kept awhile to the open water, cruising restlessly about, as he had done before in the creek and mere, raising himself at times and gazing round, as wild a looking creature as imagination can conjure up. Thence he passed into the thick fringe of reeds, and remained hidden so long that it might be thought that he had laid up there. Later however he appeared on the far bank of the west-ernmost pool, and though the pale primrose streak in the east warned him of coming day, the outlawed animal, alarmed by the taint of human footprints he had happened on, at once forsook the refuge and set his face for the marsh.

His hurried movements showed that he had full knowledge of the risk he ran in the open, where he looked a monster as he crossed the patches of sward amongst the bilberry. Indeed, so fast did he cover the ground that no sprinter could have kept up with him, especially when he breasted the long, boulder-strewn ascent to the Kites' Cairn. There old Ikey must have viewed him had he been on his way to the pools at his usual hour; but he was late, and soon the otter was amongst the crags. His feet were here delayed momentarily by the rising sun, whose light he dreaded as much as did the witches of Crowz-an-Wra. But there was no staying where he was: he must press on to marsh or sea, now both in his view; and at a panic speed he made his way down the bare slope and up the opposite rise to the great furze brake that runs down almost to the margin of the mere. Leisurely he threaded his way through the close cover to a point where he stood and listened to the crowing of a cock before slipping into the water and crossing to the old hover on the edge of the reed-bed. He made his careful toilet as usual, and before the marshman discovered his tracks he had curled up and fallen asleep.

But whilst the otter slept in untroubled security, heedless of his enemies, they had passed the Liddens and come within earshot of the old man, who had scarcely finished his soliloquy when he started to his feet with the exclamation, 'What's that?' and stood listening as intently as the otter a little earlier had listened for a reply to his call. This time, however, the reply came. 'Surely theere

'tes again', and a few seconds later, as the cry rose afresh, he shouted "Tes they' so loudly that he attracted the child who joined him
on the furze-rick he had hurriedly climbed.

'Do 'ee hear them, Mary? 'Tes the hounds. Hark! Cheeld.'

'I hear something, granfer.'

'Wheere do 'ee make the cry to come from?' and for answer
she pointed with her free hand to the Kites' Cairn. 'Now keep an
eye on the rocks, and tell me if you see anythin'.'

'There's something streaming through the Fairies' Gap this
minit . . . Now it's like a shadow, a moving shadow on the down . . .
They're dogs. My word, such a passel of them, all in a bunch!'

Then they passed from sight and the weird cry almost died
away; but presently the chorus swelled, and swelled, and swelled,
and then the old man saw the hounds, like maddened things,
come pouring over the brow and enter the brake full in his view.

'You're trembling', granfer.'

'Iss, cheeld, all of a quake, like the yellow furze where the
hounds are forcin' a way. The moosic is 'most too much for me.'

'Mary,' said he, and the child raised her wondering eyes to the
excited face, ' 'tes the line of the King Oter they're spakin' to, and –
who can tell? – maybe the sun will shut down on a great day. But,
lor me! what am I doin' here on this rick, with hounds about to take
the water? My place is in the *Mary Jane*.' With that he scrambled
down the rude ladder and bustled towards the spot where he had
left the boat in the early morning.

As soon as he stepped in, the pack, which had been almost
mute since entering the mere, broke out into a babel of music,
proclaiming a find. The uproar so unnerved him that he was
long in getting the oars between the thole-pins; but when he did,
he pulled with might and main till, drawing near the hounds, he

144

stopped rowing and kept a sharp lookout for the quarry repeating as he scanned the water: 'Ef 'tes only he, only he.' But not a sign of otter, big or small, met his eyes, either in the mere or in the creek, to which the chase presently shifted. There the fear that the game would land and reach the cliff suddenly possessed him. So all at once he urged the boat past hounds and island to the reedy corner, where he jumped to his feet and kept splashing the water to drive the otter back. The nearer the hounds approached the more frantically he wielded the oar, nor did he desist till they showed by their movements that the otter had left the end of the creek and was returning to the mere.

Whilst he watched them the squire and his followers came over the brow, and all made for the beach except the squire, who came tearing down the hill towards the boat.

'To the hounds, John!' he gasped as he stepped into the crazy craft. At the word the old man pushed off and bent to his work with wondrous vigour.

'Have you viewed the otter?'

'No. sir, I haven't, but I spurred un.'

'You spurred him? When?'

'Soon aifter break o' day.'

'You did?'

'Iss, sir, sure as you're standin' on they starn sheets.'

'What! the big otter?'

'Iss, sir. The King Oter, I call him.'

'Then why didn't you bring word?'

'I did, sir, fast as I could, but you'd gone off to the revur. 'Twas Mr. Pugmore as told me.'

'I see, I see! Pull with your right, or we shall be into the island. That will do; now both together.'

'Wind him, my lads! middy ho, wind him! Padzepaw, Troubadour, Rowter, wind him! Wind him, my lads!'

The cheery cry seemed to put fresh life into the hounds as they worked the reeds, from which they presently drove the quarry to the mere.

The squire's keen eyes searched the glittering surface to get a glimpse of him, but in vain; the hounds might have been giving tongue to some phantom quarry for all that he or the old man saw. And so the chase continued for an hour, and another and another, whilst the otter led the pack from reed-bed to reed-bed, where he rose and vented without exposing himself.

At last the marshman, who at the moment was resting on the oars, pointed to the surface beneath the right blade.

'The chain, the chain!' whispered the squire excitedly on sighting the string of bubbles, and 'There he vents!' as the nose of the quarry showed between two lily-leaves a few yards off. The otter remained where he was until the hounds were almost upon him; then he sank as noiselessly as he had risen, and made for another refuge.

'You viewed him, sir?'

'I viewed an otter, John.'

'Then why didn't 'ee tally him, sir?'

'Because I'm not sure it's him. I don't want to raise false hopes in all these people.'

For by this time many had arrived, some by boat, others in vehicles, some on horses or donkeys, and had taken up stations round the mere. There were at least a score on the point, as many near the inflow: there was a tall thin man who had somehow found his way to the edge of the reed-bed, and quite a little crowd on the bar.

'Never see'd such a passel o' people here since the wreck of the
Triton, and that was afore your time, sir. The casks of rum were
all over the beach, and men, too; and as for the cocoanuts, they
were . . .' The outstretched hand of the squire silenced him, for the
otter had risen within a few yards of the boat, and lay there showing its great length. Both were tongue-tied by the sight, but no
sooner did the otter dive than the squire gave utterance to a 'Tally-
ho!' the like of which had never passed his lips before. It made the
marshman jump: it sent a thrill through the cordon of spectators:
it made the child hurry again to the furze-rick.

'Did you see him?' asked the squire excitedly.

'I did, and I don't wonder it fetched such a screech out of 'ee. Lor,
maister, 'twere enow to wake the dead.'

Two minutes later the otter was 'gazed' by the men on the
point. Soon after a shout came from Geordie at the end of the
creek, – so soon that the squire feared there must be two otters
afloat. But he was wrong: there was only one. Next the people on
the bar saw him rise, with the hounds close behind driving him
towards the reed-bed, where he landed within a dozen yards of the
solitary figure there. To him it looked as if the otter must be overhauled, and eagerly he watched the swaying of the reeds as otter
and hounds traversed the bed. Soon, in view of the excited crowd
near the inflow, the hunted beast managed to slip into the mere as
a hound was about to seize him. Four times he rose in crossing to
the farther shore, where he threaded the sags and, in his desperation, sought the refuge of the furze-brake. The cover was all in his
favour; for he could run where the hounds, and even the terriers,
had to force a way. Yet to him as to them the atmosphere was suf-
focating, so that he was glad to reach the upper edge and get a few
breaths of fresh air before the clamour of the hounds and the

crackling of the stems warned him it was time to move. Then he made his way down to the creek to quench his thirst. The parson, by this time perched on the willow, saw him lapping, but forbore to shout, and presently the dark mask was withdrawn. Soon the hounds reached the spot. Thirsty though they were, they thirsted still more for the otter's blood. Not one stayed to lap but, like infuriated creatures, went on after the quarry whose distress they must have been conscious of.

Before this the crowd from the bar had moved to the bluff above the creek, whence they could trace the windings of the otter by the movements of the hounds. Breathless was their excitement when they saw from the wild shaking of the bushes that the otter had been seized, and great their disappointment when the resumption of the chase showed that, after all, he had got away.

Twice more the gallant beast made the wide circuit of those ten acres of furze in the hope of shaking off his pursuers before he made his way in despair down to the sags and slipped unseen into the mere. He rose after but a short dive, and swam with the pack in his wake straight for the bar. Not one of those who watched dreamt he would dare to land; but he did, a good score yards in front of the leading hounds. Then all could see his distress as he laboured over the pebbly ridge he knew so well. It looked as if he must be overtaken before he reached the tide; but the hounds were nearly as exhausted as he, and though they gained on him, it was not until they came to the calm water beyond the breaking wave that they managed to hold him and worry his life out.

Then the squire waded into the sea almost to his armpits, took him from the hounds, and holding the heavy carcass above his head, brought it ashore. The 'field' closed round him in their eagerness to see and touch the beast and examine the huge pads.

148

'A little elbow-room, gentlemen, if you please. I can't possibly weigh the animal whilst you press me like this.'

His words had instant effect. The moment the crowd fell back he suspended the otter from the hook of the spring-balance he carried, and watched the index.

'What does he scale, sir?' shouted a score excited voices.

'Twenty-nine pounds good.'

Then followed a tumult of conversation, amidst which could be distinguished:

'Now, Thomas 'Enery, what did I say all along?'

'He's a pound over and above your guess.'

'Sandy was right.'

'You said forty pound, Geordie, you know you did.'

'You'm a liard; I —'

'Silence, mates!' roared the landlord, stepping into the ring; 'the squire wants to spake. Silence, I say!'

When the noisy groups of disputants at last quieted down, the squire, hoarse from his efforts, said: 'It is my custom, as you know, to distribute the pads, mask and rudder, and fling the carcass to the hounds. To-day, however, I mean to depart from the rule. I will tell you why, and I hope every one of you will agree that I am right. My view is that this fine beast' – and here he lifted the otter clear of the sand as if to emphasize his words – 'which has excited so much interest and afforded a hunt we can never expect to see the like of, ought not to be broken up, but should be preserved for ourselves and others to look at in the years to come. Now, if any man has got anything to say, let him speak out.'

'Say, sir,' replied the parish clerk, after casting his quick eyes round the circle of approving faces, 'why, that we're one and all of the same way of thinkin' as yoursel'! What's a pad here or a pad there? To say nawthin' as to who's to have 'em. By all manner o' means let the otter be set up, and let un be given pride of place again' the wainscot; for if ever wild crittur deserved the honour, this one do, if only for the good he's done the landlord.'

So the otter was set up in the hall in a handsome case, with a picture of the marsh for background. Of the many trophies that adorn the walls there is not one the squire was so proud of, none whose story he liked so well to relate. It alone bears no inscription; for, as he always said, 'There is no need; my people will never let the record die!' His words have proved true.

Though the wild promontory is steeped in legend and romance, though tales of giants, fairies, smugglers and ship-wrecked sailors, abound, there is no story the crofters so often repeat by the firelight as the story of the otter, none the children listen to with closer attention. Mary's three boys never wearied of hearing their mother tell how she stood on the rick and watched the hounds stream through the Fairies' Gap; they always insisted on her giving the squire's 'Tally ho!' and hung on every word when she came to the message brought by the steward, that old John and his grandchild were to have their little place rent free for the rest of their days.

'Again, again!' they would cry, clapping their little hands; and generally Mary yielded to their entreaties. And when the time comes they will repeat the tale to their own children, as indeed do the miller's and the moorman's sons and daughters to-day. Thus the tradition of the otter bids fair to be handed on by generation after generation for long years to come, and to win an imperish-able place amongst the hearthside stories of the West.

OTTER
CONSERVATION

ᥰᴄ

CORNWALL WILDLIFE TRUST

Cornwall Wildlife Trust manages over 50 nature reserves around Cornwall that are open to the public. Its aim is to protect these land and marine habitats and their associated flora and fauna, as well as protecting special geological sites. It is the only organisation solely concerned with all aspects of wildlife conservation in Cornwall and fulfils a role occupied by no other countryside organisation.

Together with 47 other local Wildlife Trusts throughout the country, Cornwall Wildlife Trust encourages people to enjoy nature and increase their understanding of the environment. It does this through a range of workshops, events, walks and talks. It has a number of specialist groups and many keen volunteers working on a variety of conservation projects.

One of these specialist groups is the Cornwall Otter Group and Cornwall can boast of an increasing number of 'otter spotters'. Dedicated volunteers become part of the Cornwall Otter Group and are trained to detect otter tracks and signs and to help monitor sites. These volunteers are an invaluable part of Water for Wildlife (formerly the Otters and Rivers Project). Water for Wildlife has a strong advisory role with a wide range of landowners and organisations to address vital issues such as wetland habitat loss, disturbance or creation, otter predation and one of the biggest threats – otters killed on roads. Collecting these corpses for post-mortem, at Britain's first ever Wildlife Veterinary Investigation Centre in Cornwall, is a priority, as so much can be learnt about their age, sex, breeding and health status. The centre was set up in partnership with Cornwall Wildlife Trust. The objectives of the centre are to investigate incidents of wildlife mortality; to monitor the health status of wildlife; and to examine healthy specimens and build a database of normal values.

To become involved with the work of the Cornwall Wildlife Trust, visit www.cornwallwildlifetrust.org.uk or telephone 01872 273939.

To become a member of Cornwall Wildlife Trust, and so become involved in all these activities, telephone 01872 240777 or e-mail Andrea Toy, andrea@cornwt.demon.co.uk

For further information on otters, becoming an otter spotter or joining the Otter Group, contact Kate Stokes, kate@cornwt.demon.co.uk

THE OTTER TRUST

The Otter Trust is a registered charity whose main aim is to encourage the conservation of otters throughout the world, but with particular emphasis on the European Otter. An important part of its work was the re-introduction of otters to the wild in co-operation with English Nature.

The Otter Trust manages five wildlife wetland reserves. Three of the reserves are open to visitors; details appear below. To contribute to the work of the Otter Trust or to find out more, visit the website at www.ottertrust.org.uk or telephone 01986 893470.

THE MAMMAL SOCIETY

The Mammal Society works to protect British mammals, halt the decline of threatened species and advise on all issues affecting British mammals. It studies mammals, identifies the problems they face and promotes conservation.

To contribute to the work of The Mammal Society or for more information on its network of volunteers, visit the website at www.abdn.ac.uk/mammal or telephone 020 7350 2200.

THE INTERNATIONAL OTTER SURVIVAL FUND

The IOSF was set up to protect and help the 13 species of otter worldwide through a combination of compassion and science. It supports projects to protect otters through practical conservation, education and research, and the rescue and rehabilitation of sick and orphaned otters. To contribute to the work of the International Otter Survival Fund or to find out more, visit the website at www.otter.org or telephone 01471 822487.

OTTER HABITATS

Cornwall provides the full range of habitats required by the otter in freshwater in the south-west, from upland headwaters to lowland reaches. Otters need high water quality, good fish stocks and areas of undisturbed riparian vegetation such as scrub and wet meadows, all of which are available in the county.

When the total otter population was at a national low point, otters remained in Cornwall and Devon, although in lower numbers, and rivers such as the Camel and Fowey maintained relatively healthy populations. It was from those river catchments that the otter populations have once again spread out and otters are now believed to be present in river catchments throughout Cornwall.

The river Camel is of international importance and as such is classified as a Special Area of Conservation (SAC), as well as a Site of a Special Scientific Interest (SSSI).

The Environment Agency is the lead organisation for Otters under the UK Biodiversity Action Plan. Through the Environment Agency's core environmental protection, the habitats and food for otters are maintained and improved. Successful partnership projects with English Nature, Cornwall Wildlife Trust and Pennon Group (South West Water) have also raised public awareness and protected and restored habitats. This includes the funding of a specific Otter Project officer and a large amount of research into levels of pesticide residue in otter carcasses.

The majority of the otter corpses analysed have been collected from road deaths that are now considered to be the greatest cause of mortality for otters. The number of otters killed on the road has been increasing over the past decade. This is actually a good sign that otter numbers are increasing and the population is increasing its range across the UK. The Environment Agency works with the Highways Agency and local authorities to ensure that special otter crossings are provided at road death hot spots.

The otter population in Cornwall is healthy and still increasing, although this increase is slowing as population numbers reach their upper limits.

WHERE TO SEE OTTERS

• In the West Country you can visit the Otter Trust's Tamar Otter Sanctuary (from April to October) at North Petherwin, five miles east of Launceston, Cornwall.
Telephone 01566 785646.

• In East Anglia you can visit the Otter Trust at Earsham, near Bungay, Suffolk.
Telephone 01986 893470.

• In the North of England you can visit the Otter Trust's North Pennines Reserve at Vale House Farm, Near Bowes, Barnard Castle, County Durham.
Telephone 01833 628339.

• Elsewhere in England, the New Forest Otter, Owl and Wildlife Park is a Conservation Park set in 25 acres of ancient woodland within the New Forest Heritage area. For more information visit the website at www.ottersandowls.co.uk
Telephone 02380 292408.

• The Chestnut Centre Otter, Owl and Wildlife Centre, near Chapel-en-le-Frith, Derbyshire, has four species of otter. For more information visit the website at www.ottersandowls.co.uk
Telephone 01298 814099.

GLOSSARY

❧

B

beetling	cliff with an overhang
bluff	steep, broad-fronted cliff
blunderbuss	short, large-bored gun for short-range use
boles	trunks of trees
bosky	wooded or bushy
bra	very, or good
brae	steep bank or hillside
brake	thicket that can provide cover for wildlife
brigantine	sailing ship with two masts

C

cairn	mound of rough stones built as a monument or landmark
cheeld	child
clitter	loose boulders or stones
cotter	farm labourer or cottage tenant
couching	to lie, especially in a lair
crittur	creature
crofter	farmer of a small-holding or 'croft'
cromlech	dolmen: a megalithic tomb
curley	curlew

D

dace	freshwater fish related to the carp
demesne	landed estate or property

E

enow	enough
eyot	small island, particularly in a river

F

faggots	bundles of sticks for the fire
flintlock	old gun that is fired by a spark from a flint
freshet	rush of fresh water flowing into the sea
furze	gorse

G

granfer	grandfather
grilse	young salmon that has returned to fresh water from the sea for the first time
groat	obsolete small silver coin of four old pence

H

hieing	hurrying
holt	animal's, especially an otter's, lair

I

iss	yes

K

killick	small anchor for boats

M

mace-reed	freshwater plant
marches	boundary lines
may-horn	large tin horn traditionally blown by boys on

	May Day
medlar-tree	tree bearing small, brown, apple-like fruit, which is eaten when half rotten
mere	lake or pool
morass	bog or marsh

N

neddy	donkey

O

osier	willow

P

passel	a large number
passun	parson
peel	small inedible fish
piskies	the little people
pollack	cod-like fish usually found near river locks
pollard	tree that is regularly cut back to encourage new growth
purlieus	boundaries or limits of land

Q

quoit	the flat stone of a dolmen, or megalithic tomb

R

reeve	the chief magistrate of a town or district
revur	river
rick	stack of hay, corn or furze

S

scrimmage	a brawl
sett	badger's lair
sexton	person who looks after a church and church-yard, often responsible for grave-digging
smack	single-masted sailing-boat for coasting or fishing
spindrift	spray blown along the surface of the sea
spraints	otter droppings
strame	stream
sward	expanse of short grass

T

tarn	small mountain lake
teasy	irritable
thole-pin	pin in the gunwhale of a boat at the fulcrum, for oars
throstle	song thrush
tithe	one tenth of the annual produce of land
toothsome	delicious
trimmer	short piece of timber across an opening
turbot	edible flatfish

V

varmint	vermin

W

welkin	the sky
welter	confused

wheatear songbird with a black tail and white rump

whiffing-line fishing line that is towed so that the bait appears to be a living fish

will-o'-the-wisp phosphorescent light seen on marshy ground

withy willow

wrack seaweed cast up or growing on the shore

wrasse brightly coloured sea fish with thick lips and strong teeth